In memorium
The Bridge, Canoe, Columbia, Finlay, Kootenay,
Nechako, Parsnip, Peace.......
rivers lost to Hydroelectric power projects.

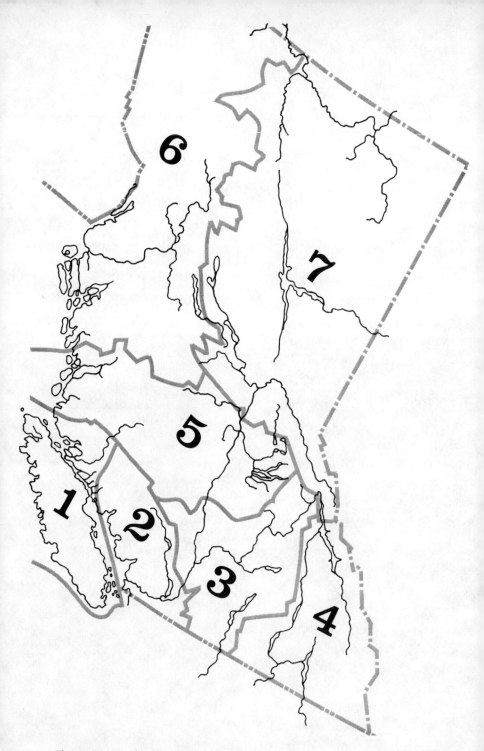

The regions on this map have been adapted from the divisions used in the **British Columbia Recreational Atlas**

REGIONAL INDEX

INTRODUCTION

British Columbia is a land of abundant waters - creeks, rivers, lakes, ocean. The variety of terrain provides forms of water to satisfy a diversity of needs and functions. Voyageurs who historically used waterways as a means of transportation were one of the non-consumptive users of rivers and were the forerunners of a modern day sport. Canoeing has come into popularity as a form of recreation, and is considered one of the lifetime sports for it can be taught to the young, and enjoyed at any age, varying the physical effort to suit the individual. Exercise or relaxation, excitement or peacefulness, companionship or solitude - the pleasures and challenges to the canoeist are as varied as the waters to be traversed.

This publication is a where-to rather than a how-to book, for there are already many fine books available by experts on the techniques and skills required in canoeing. Many of these are listed in the Bibliography, but there are two books that we have found particularly helpful which we feel are worthy of special mention. Our own introduction to canoeing was Bill Riviere's *Pole, Paddle & Portage, A Complete Guide to Canoeing,* which is a good basic paddling book. For those who are into wilderness canoeing, a recent publication, *The Complete Wilderness Paddler* by James West Davidson and John Rugge, is both helpful and presented in an interesting manner. We also recommend that a basic paddling course be taken to facilitate learning some of the skills involved in canoeing.

The routes compiled in this book are intended to be a comprehensive guide to the water courses of British Columbia. Though written with the canoeist in mind, some of the data will be useful to rafters and kayakers; however the routes have been included only if some part of the route is used for canoeing. The information is as complete and up-to-date as possible, but is not meant to be the only source of reference. For example detailed maps have purposely been excluded from the book since we feel that obtaining topo maps is critical to safety in navigating rivers and travelling in the wilderness. The maps included are simply to give a general idea of the courses of rivers, and of the position of lake chains in relationship to the areas in which they are located. Additional suggestions of reading material relating to specific areas have been included within the route descriptions.

The limited details regarding flora, fauna, history and geology which are found in the route descriptions are included to whet the appetite; for we believe that part of the fun in travelling a route is in discovering things for oneself.

Along with the routes we have prepared a section on safety, since we feel a responsibility to those who we may be encouraging to get out onto the water. However we can only write these things down - it is up to the individual to arm himself or herself with the knowledge and equipment on which lives may depend.

The compiling and writing of this canoe trip guide was much more difficult than had been anticipated. Not for a lack of routes, or a lack of enthusiasm, but because during the whole course of the project our weathered 17 foot prospector Chestnut sat across two saw horses an arm's length from the typewriter. And it needed a lot of work. Last summer while on a journey across the prairies, a gale snapped the tie-downs and bounced it along the highway. Emergency repairs made it floatable, but it needed a few ribs and planks patched and some rather extensive canvas repairs. It was often a test of will power to decide which was the most important, a book on canoe routes, or the canoe; and each time we researched a new back country journey it seemed to be more urgent to get those patches on. How can one write about the West Road or Dease, or remember the Chilko-Chilcotin or Fort Nelson with a holed canoe close at hand? Even researching the trips seemed to steal time from the actual writing. How many complete trips or expeditions have we planned and practically canoed while writing? When could we take that trip? This May, or June? And the longer one in fly country, perhaps August, just after we revisit the Stuart River country and the Nechako? The canoeing clinic on the Thompson? Well perhaps we could squeeze that in during June sometime, or July. And then next year, and the year after. So many waters to paddle, so many places to see in this province. Most of the trips are recorded here. Now if we can just get that final coat of paint on....

Richard Wright
Rochelle Wright
Port Moody, B.C.

HISTORY

The history of canoeing in British Columbia is really the story of the development of our province, for the geography of the land made river travel the natural way to open up the country. Even those who journeyed by land were constantly faced with rivers to cross.

It is theorized that the earliest people in North America arrived by crossing the Bering Strait. The native Indians who then inhabited the west depended on canoes for transport, hunting, fishing and trading. When the early white explorers arrived on the scene, with their journals providing some of our earliest written history, they admired the fine seaworthy canoes made by the Indians. The explorations which followed were generally accomplished by canoe, almost exclusively by full time fur-traders. Some of the early travellers and immigrants to British Columbia also arrived by boat. The Cariboo gold seekers ran the Fraser and Thompson Rivers in a variety of rafts, bullboats and dugout canoes; the Klondikers used rivercraft to pass through British Columbia on their way to the Yukon gold fields. When the railway came, the steel rails were laid across land that had been chained, surveyed, mapped and even partly settled by people in canoes.

Provincial Archives, B.C.

Provincial Archives, B.C.

More recent pioneers and adventurers used canoes, freighters and scows to take them into country which wasn't serviced by railways and highways. As recently as the Second World War, scows and freighters were used on the Dease River; and until the Hart Highway was opened in 1952, the Crooked River was still used for freighting into the north. R.M. Patterson, whose stories still enthuse canoeists, paddled and lined his way up and down many rivers such as the Dease, the Finlay and the Nahanni.

The dangers of river travel were much greater in the early days of limited communications with few maps and books, or guides to consult. Also early travellers did not have the benefit of life jackets, and many did not know how to swim. When the Overlanders arrived at the Upper Fraser and contemplated rafting and canoeing it, they knew only that the Hudson's Bay Company had used boats on it some years previously. Even the Indians knew little of the river below except that there were canyons and rapids. As the adventurers headed down the river, the Indians commented, "Poor white men no more". A few did lose their lives but most survived, enriched with experiences of the territory that was to become for some of them their new home.

Canoeing as a means of recreation has surged to popularity during the 60's and 70's as more and more people have been searching out forms of sport which give relief from the pressures of urban living and from an increased dependence on machines in other aspects of their lives. Canoeing has also become an ideal way to relive some of the history of British Columbia and to recapture the sense of adventure experienced by some of our forefathers.

CLASSIFICATION OF RIVERS

The classification of rivers according to a standard can be valuable as a general guide to the navigability of the river. However all water bodies including rivers are living, moving, changing entities which vary with the weather and the seasons. It is difficult therefore to grade rivers without elaborating on all the possible variations and changes.

The recognized standard for the grading of rivers is the International River Classification. We have used this grading system for our routes, based on the most recent and accurate information that we could obtain.

This standard of classification does have some limitations which should be taken into consideration by the canoeist. The International Classification is based on easy access and egress and average water levels; it does not make allowances for loaded canoes and cold water. So in a wilderness situation, the dangers associated with a graded section of water may be increased where help is not readily available, and may make unrunnable that which could easily be done in a controlled situation. For example an experienced paddler who was normally capable of handling a Grade 3 rapid may only be able to cope with Grade 2 water with a loaded canoe, where cold water and difficult access make a spill too risky. Another limitation of this system is in the grading of large volume rivers such as the Fraser, where the volume provides a powerful force with boils and souse holes, which can be dangerous even within a Grade 1 section of water. The final consideration in classification is to understand that a rise or fall in the level of the river can alter the grade of a section of river within a very short period of time.

The International River Classification

The following interpretation of the International River Classification is made by Canoe Sport British Columbia.

Grade 1
Easy. Waves small and regular; passages clear; occasional sand banks and artificial difficulties like bridge piers. Suitable for novices in closed canoes, kayaks and open Canadians.

Grade 2
Quite easy. Rapids of medium difficulty; passages clear and wide. Occasional boulders in stream. Suitable for intermediate paddlers in closed canoes, kayaks and open Canadians.

Grade 3
Medium difficulty. Waves numerous, high, irregular. Rocks and narrow (clear) passages. Considerable experience in maneuvering required. Advance scouting usually needed. Canoes will ship water, and unless equipped with spray covers, will require frequent emptying. Kayaks must be equipped with spray covers. Suitable for experienced paddlers in closed canoes and kayaks, and expert paddlers in open Canadians.

Grade 4

Difficult. Long rapids, powerful irregular waves; dangerous rocks, boiling eddies; passages difficult to reconnoitre; advance scouting mandatory; powerful and precise maneuvering required. Spray decks mandatory. Suitable for expert closed canoes and kayaks only. Not suitable for open Canadian canoes.

Grade 5

Very difficult. Extremely demanding long and very violent rapids, following each other almost without interruption. River bed extremely obstructed; big drops; very steep gradient; advance scouting mandatory and usually difficult due to nature of terrain. Suitable for expert paddlers only in closed canoes and kayaks with specific white water training under expert leadership. Not suitable for open Canadian canoes.

Grade 6

Extraordinarily difficult. The difficulties of Grade 5 carried to extremes. Nearly impossible and very dangerous. Suitable for teams of expert paddlers only in closed boats at favourable water levels and after careful study, with fully trained and experienced rescue team in position. Not suitable for open Canadian canoes.

CANOEING SAFETY

There are two aspects of safety to be considered by the canoeist - safety involving the water itself and survival in a remote or wilderness situation. The following pages cover the basic safety considerations for canoeists including some general rules for water and wilderness safety, a discussion of equipment and some first aid measures. It is recommended that the individual continue his or her own research by doing further reading or perhaps taking a course on canoeing or survival. Suggestions for supplementary reading are contained in the bibliography and contacts for classes can be found in the appendices.

Safety and Survival

Preparing oneself for a safe canoeing outing involves being well trained, knowledgeable and adequately equipped for the trip to be undertaken. The following are recognized rules for outdoor safety which relate to the canoeing experience

— Never canoe alone; for any trip into back country or a wilderness area, there should be a minimum of three canoes.
— Wear a life jacket, which has been tested.
— Learn paddling skills in a controlled situation.
— Know your own abilities and limitations.
— Be in good physical condition before attempting a long or difficult trip.
— **Leave word with a responsible person indicating where you are going** to canoe and when you expect to return; report back to them on your return. In Provincial or National Parks, leave word at the park office or with a park's official; in wilderness areas contact the R.C.M.P.
— Carry emergency supplies, including extra food, change of clothing, canoe repair kit, first aid kit and survival equipment. (More details on emergency supplies are included in the section on equipment.)

- Watch for changes in the weather, and always be prepared for wind and rain.
- In case of sudden bad weather, find shelter.
- Keep dry and warm and watch each other for signs of fatigue or hypothermia. (More information on this condition is included in the section on hypothermia.)
- Be aware of changes in the river level causing rivers to be more swift and hazardous.
- Scout unfamiliar rivers by land in advance and note any hazards such as rapids, rocks, gravel bars, deadheads, sweepers or log jams.
- Go through rapids or hazardous spots one canoe at a time, allowing each one room to maneuver and putting only one boat at a time into a vulnerable position.
- Travel close to shore on lakes or in the ocean.
- Obtain tide information where applicable, and be aware of currents.
- Know and practice rescue techniques.
- In case of a spill: stay with the canoe, unless your life is endangered by rapids ahead or by the cold water; assist other canoeists where possible; hang onto the upstream end of the canoe to keep it between you and any hazards; try to swim the canoe to shore.

Priorities of Survival

In the event of making a decision to stay put and wait for rescue or wait out a storm, it is important to understand the priorities necessary to survival:
1. State of mind
2. Air
3. Shelter
4. Water
5. Food

The will to live and to think rationally through a problem without panicking gives a person the best possible chance of surviving any situation. The conservation of energy should be a key factor in making decisions. For example, swimming a long distance to shore is likely to be more of any energy drain than staying with a boat and gradually drifting and swimming it to shore; and searching for edible plants for food may use up more calories than it supplies.

Leader Responsibilities

Whenever a group of people are out canoeing together there should be someone who is designated as the leader to carry out the following responsibilities:
— Have good prior knowledge of the route to be canoed.
— Ascertain that the trip to be undertaken is not beyond the capability of any participant.
— Have preknowledge of medical problems and allergies of every member of the group.
— Be sure that each member is suitably clothed and equipped.
— Have knowledge of local weather conditions and probable changes in water levels.
— Proceed at the speed of the slowest participant.
— Keep the group together.
— Be willing to stop or turn back in case of hazardous weather or other problems.
— Monitor the physical conditions of members of the group.
— Make decisions relating to safety.
— Supervise rescue operations.

Equipment

The discussion of equipment here will primarily take the form of a list of gear to be considered for canoe outings, with a few comments, notes and hints included.

First though, here are some suggestions regarding the choosing of a canoe outfit. There is no best choice for any one person or any one situation. Individual preferences will vary according to the kind of canoeing to be done, the ruggedness and durability required in a canoe, finances, and personal taste. The basic equipment required is a canoe, paddles, and life jackets.

Since there are many variables it is wise to research what is available and what will best suit your requirements. Suggestions of ways to begin this research are:
— Read what the experts have to say about choosing equipment; several books in the bibliography include this kind of information.
— Talk to experienced canoeists; if you don't know any personally, check with one of the canoe clubs.
— Check out a minimum of two stores - if you deal with someone who is a canoeist, you are likely to get more knowledgeable assistance; avoid peak busy times to get the most help.
— Try renting different types of equipment; however it may be difficult to rent some things, such as a wood and canvas canoe (which requires more upkeep).
— Take a canoe course - canoes are usually provided giving the participant an opportunity to try out equipment with the added advantage of being able to obtain advice from the instructor.

Accoutrements to be considered when choosing a canoe include a keel, a platform which will hold an outboard motor, a sail, and a pole. Also you will need a roof rack or some method of transporting the canoe.

Care of the canoe and its accessories takes some time and effort but pays off with fewer problems on the water, and longer service over the years. A few hints on protection, storage and maintenance follow:

— Fasten the canoe well while transporting it; having watched our own canoe blow off the van in a heavy wind and bounce down the road behind, we feel constrained to remind others to not only tie the canoe down well, but to also check the ropes and ties frequently.
— Avoid dragging over rocks or gravel bars.
— Have canoe parallel to shore and properly afloat while being loaded.
— Step into the water to board and leave a canoe at the water's edge, as wet feet are preferable to a scraped bottom.
— Swish each foot in water to rinse off sand and gravel when stepping into the boat.
— Lift canoe onto shore for overnight stops or if there are large waves.
— Store protected from extremes of weather - rain, snow, hot sun - preferably indoors; canoes can be suspended with ropes or on a rack; wood and canvas should not be turned upside down on the ground for any length of time unless set on boards, as dry rot is likely to set in where the canoe touches the ground.
— Store paddles by hanging or suspending to prevent warping.
— Store life jackets in a dry airy place.
— Maintain equipment in good order; keep surfaces well sanded and painted or varnished.

Basic Equipment

— Canoe - wood and canvas, fibreglass and aluminum are the main canoe types used in this area; should be tested before embarking on a long trip.
— Bow and stern lines or painters - should be attached to both ends of the canoe, rolled up neatly, but quickly available when needed; a floating type line 30-50 mm by a minimum of 5 metres is recommended (up to 30 metres may be required for lining or tracking a canoe).
— Spray covers - frequently used on open canoes in white water to keep waves out; are also useful in protecting gear in rainy weather, and to keep warmth in and wind out in cold weather.
— Paddles - one for each paddler plus a spare tied in but readily available for use.
— Life jackets - one for each person in the canoe; test while fully clothed - must be capable of supporting an unconscious person in face up position; should be worn at all times in a boat by children and non-swimmers, and should be worn by everyone whenever there is a chance of an upset.
— Knee pads - may be needed for comfort; never use life jackets to kneel on.
— Map and compass - important to know how to use.
— Matches in waterproof container (35 mm film cans are watertight) or firestarter.
— Knife - axe or saw may also be included.
— Shelter material.
— Food, utensils and cleaning items.

— Stove and fuel - not always necessary but advisable in parks or on longer trips where there may be some fire restrictions.
— Clothing suitable to the season.
— Change of clothing.
— Rain gear.
— Toilet articles.
— Toilet paper.
— Sun glasses.
— Sun protection cream.
— Lip ointment
— Insect repellent.

First Aid Kit (in waterproof container)
— Butterfly tapes, gauze pads, tape, elastoplast bandage, tensors, slings, scissors, tweezers, safety pins, needle, antiseptic, vaseline, thermometer, salt tablets, pain medication, antiallergenic medication, personal medications, snake bite kit, calamine or zinc oxide lotion.

Canoe Repair Kit
— For wood and canvas tears this should include canvas patches and plastic resin marine glue; structural repairs are more complicated but can usually be improvised using a knife and sticks or wood available in the vicinity.
— Fiberglass repair kits should include fibreglass patching material and epoxy.
— Aluminum is less likely to require patching but more difficult to repair; temporary patching may be attempted with roofing cement or with a cloth patch glued with pitch or cement.

Survival Kit
— In addition to the basic equipment already mentioned, the following should be put into a compact watertight container and fastened to the belt of each canoeist.

— Map and compass, matches, knife, paper, pencil, signalling mirror, whistle, space blanket, snare wire, fishing kit, tinfoil (for cooking), emergency food rations eg. bouillon cubes, soup, tea, sugar, chocolate, salt.

Equipment for Overnight or longer trips
— Sleeping bags, ensolite foam pads for insulation, tent or tarp.

For carrying equipment in canoes, a few large packs are better than a lot of small containers; this is especially appreciated when loading and unloading the canoe, and when carrying over a portage. Ammunition boxes with rubber gaskets come in a variety of sizes and make ideal watertight containers for cameras and film, first aid kits and repair kits. Heavy plastic laundry bags can be used to protect sleeping bag rolls.

Clothing

Clothing for canoeing should be chosen for comfort and safety rather than fashion. It should keep the individual dry and warm or cool and protected from the sun. As a general guideline clothing should provide good insulation, allow moisture to evaporate, be light, adaptable to changes in the weather or activity, and allow freedom of movement.

The system of dressing to best suit the above requirements is called layering. This involves wearing several layers of lightweight clothing which can be removed or added to keep warm or cool. Each layer serves to trap air and body heat. Wool clothing is recommended when it is cold, as wool retains insulating quality when wet to a much greater degree than any other kind of fabric. And wet clothes increase susceptibility to hypothermia due to heat loss. Layered clothing can be easily removed to prevent sweating and quickly donned when taking a rest or if a wind comes up.

The following clothing should be considered for canoeing excursions:
— Underclothing - wool recommended for chilly weather.
— Pants - wool or cotton, depending on the nature of the trip; jeans and tight pants should be avoided.
— Shirts - lightweight; long-sleeved in insect and sun country; also wool shirts for cooler weather and evenings.
— Jacket - should be windproof and lightweight; fibrefill retains insulating qualities even when wet.
— Socks - protect against cold feet and insects.
— Shoes - lightweight leather, moccasins or sneakers best in canoe; boots may also be wanted for portaging and camping.
— Hat - important for protection from wet, cold, sun and insects; up to 60% of body heat can be lost through an uncovered head.
— Gloves - may be needed on long paddles or in insect country.
— Rain suit - for keeping dry in the canoe and in camp.
— Rubber wetsuit - ideal in very cold water.
— Wetsuit socks - worth considering where there is considerable lining or tracking to do with wet feet.
— Complete change of dry clothes.

Food and Nutrition

Food is the fuel which provides the energy on which our bodies run. We require food to keep us warm and to supply energy for muscular work. Since canoeing can be a strenuous activity, caloric intake must be increased to provide energy for the physical exertion and to replace any heat loss from exposure to cold weather or water. Inadequate food intake combined with hard physical activity may cause food exhaustion, characterized by weakness, dizziness and nausea. It also makes a person more susceptible to hypothermia.

To maintain good nutrition while canoeing you should begin and end the day's activities with a substantial meal. Through the day it is best to eat frequent small meals and snacks. The powdered, dehydrated, freeze-dried foods available today are ideal to take along due to their light weight. However many of these tend to be expensive and some are of questionable palatability. Usually expense can be minimized by shopping at a large supermarket for such items as dried fruits, dried vegetables, instant rice, instant potatoes, packaged soups, powdered beverages, powdered desserts, nuts and seasonings. Packaging foods in meal-size portions in heavy plastic bags simplifies meal preparations in the outdoors. Fresh meat and vegetables can be used for the first day or two of any trip. Keep in mind too, that one of the advantages of canoeing is that you can handle more weight than with backpacking. The trick is to use the heaviest foods prior to any portages.

A word of caution for those travelling in bear country, which includes most of British Columbia: Food should never be left lying around camp or in tents. Pack it well and suspend it in a tree well away from camp. All food wastes should be burned.

Dehydration can be a problem, especially with heavy physical activity and in hot weather. Canoeists usually have little problem finding a water supply but should be sure that it is safe to drink. Contaminated water may be treated by boiling or with chemicals to render it potable. Replacement of electrolytes such as salt is equally as important as replacing fluids and can be accomplished by taking salt tablets. Inadequate replacement of fluids and salt results in a condition of heat exhaustion, with symptoms of thirst, weakness, faintness, nausea and cold clammy skin. Treatment includes rest, and a good intake of fluids and salt tablets.

Hypothermia

Hypothermia is a condition of the body in which the innercore temperature falls to a level at which the vital organs no longer function effectively. It is caused by situations in which the body loses heat faster than it produces heat. Hypothermia, known to many people as exposure, is a serious condition which will result in death if it is not recognized and treated in its earlier stages.

Normal body temperature is the result of a balance between heat production and heat loss. The primary sources of heat production are food and muscular activity, which are supplemented by external sources of heat such as the sun, a warm environment or the oral intake of hot fluids.

Equilibrium of body heat is maintained by the cooling effects of radiation, conduction, convection and by the effects of evaporation, respiration and wind.

The specific factors which lead to hypothermia in the outdoors are cold, wetness, wind and fatigue. Since it is not uncommon for a canoeist to be confronted by a combination of these conditions it is vitally important that all canoeists be able to recognize the symptoms of hypothermia and be prepared to implement prevention and treatment. It is surprising to note that most hypothermia accidents occur between -1 and 10° Celsius (30-50°F).

Symptoms of hypothermia are easily recognizable to anyone who is aware of them. Everyone will already be familiar with the early stage of hypothermia characterized by feeling cold, feeling numb and shivering. As the state of hypothermia increases the following progression of symptoms will be noted:

1. Uncontrollable shivering.
2. Continued violent shivering, vague slow slurred speech, memory lapses and incoherence.
3. Muscular rigidity, fumbling hands, frequent stumbling, lurching gait, impaired judgement and reasoning power.
4. Drowsiness, apparent exhaustion and inability to get moving after a rest, irrational behaviour, drifts into stupor, decreased pulse and respiration rate.
5. Unconsciousness, reflexes cease to function, erratic pulse.
6. Failure of cardiac and respiratory centres in brain resulting in death.

Prevention of hypothermia and its lethal sequence of symptoms begins at home with good preparations for the outdoors, and relies on alert responses to combat any problems that arise on an outing. Home preparation should include provisions for adequate rescue, clothing, shelter and emergency rations as well as a knowledge of the symptoms of hypothermia. Measures to avoid exposure include the following:

1. Dress appropriately.
2. Stay warm and dry.
   — Remove clothing before it gets wet from perspiration.
   — Put on extra clothing before you start shivering.
   — Put on rain gear before you get wet.
   — If you fall in the water, get into dry clothes and warm up before proceeding.
3. Keep rested
   — Travel at a reasonable speed.
   — Plan rest stops.
4. Maintain energy.
   — Eat nutritious meals
   — Nibble on snack foods such as nuts, dried fruit, jerky and candy between meals.
5. Be alert for signs of fatigue or symptoms of hypothermia in any member of the group.
6. Terminate exposure if you can't stay warm and dry in existing conditions.
   — Give up goal.
   — Seek shelter.
   — Build fire.
   — Camp or bivouac.

It is the nature of hypothermia that when an individual is no longer generating heat by himself, it is impossible for that person to rewarm himself; any application of heat must be provided by external sources. When progressive symptoms of hypothermia are recognized, exposure must be terminated and the following treatment begun immediately, even though the victim may deny that he needs help:

1. Get the victim out of the wind, rain and cold by providing shelter.
2. Strip off all wet clothes.
3. If mildly impaired, put into dry clothes and prewarmed sleeping bag; give warm, non-alcholic drinks and candy or other sweetened food. If semi-conscious or worse, leave stripped and put in pre-warmed sleeping bag with another person, also stripped, or in a double bag between two stripped donors; must be kept awake and given warm drinks as long as conscious.
4. Use a thermometer to determine the extent of hypothermia and to measure recovery.
5. Build a fire to warm the camp.
6. When the victim has recovered sufficiently, feed him.
7. Make sure the victim is kept warm and dry on the trip out.
8. Get medical help. It is imperative that anyone who has suffered from the effects of hypothermia be taken for a medical checkup as soon as possible, even though the victim seems completely recovered.

In addition to hypothermia, there are a few other situations requiring minor first aid which may be of particular interest to canoeists, such as sun stroke, burns, poison ivy and snake and insect bites. First though it should be stressed that all users of the outdoors should invest some time in a comprehensive first aid course. The importance of this kind of knowledge in a wilderness situation is obvious, but can also be useful when canoeing where help is nearby. For example the methods of applying artificial respiration may be needed at any time, and are best learned when they can be demonstrated and practiced under supervision.

There are, too, a few general precautions to be considered. Always carry identification, including important medical information; special medic alert bracelets can be purchased and engraved with this information. A good first aid kit is invaluable but it is of equal importance to know how to use it. The best first aid kit is one built on your own knowledge and designed for your own specific use; it should include medications and equipment to cope with personal conditions such as allergies.

In case of an accident, there is an order in which symptoms should be evaluated and treatment begun:
1. Keep calm.
2. Check respirations and give mouth to mouth artificial respiration, if breathing has stopped.
3. Check for bleeding and apply pressure to arrest it.
4. Check for injuries to head, neck and spine and for fractures or dislocations.
5. Treat shock, which is present to some degree in any case of injury.
6. Decide whether the victim may be taken to medical help, then proceed to evacuate; or send for help and provide shelter, food and care while waiting for assistance.

If someone is hurt and it is necessary to send for help, at least one person should stay with the injured party while one goes for assistance; if the group is large it is best to send two people. It is also important when sending for help in a medical emergency to write down as much as possible, such as the location, details of the extent of the injury, the name of the victim and the emergency contact at home. Where a rescue party is required, the R.C.M.P. will make the decision as to how the search and rescue is to be carried out.

Sunstroke
This is a condition which occurs when the body becomes overheated through exposure to the sun. The circulatory system has to work very hard to try and cool the body which results in a hot, flushed face, rapid pulse, weakness, dizziness and headache. Wearing a hat is the best prevention for sunstroke. Treatment includes rest out of the sun, drinking cold fluids, and a sponge with cool water. Sunstroke is not as obvious as the name implies and companions should be watched for symptoms.

Burns
Sunburns occur very readily in a water environment, and minor burns from

a campfire or hot water are other possibilities on a canoe outing. Prevention of sunburn involves gradual exposure to the sun using a sun cream; after desired period of exposure, wear long sleeved shirt long pants and a wide brimmed hat. In case of a minor burn from any cause, keep the burned area clean, out of the sun, and apply a soothing cream to keep the skin from drying. If the burn is serious enough to cause a blister or broken skin, cover the area with a sterile dressing and seek medical attention. Also take salt tablets and drink lots of fluids.

Poison Ivy

Poison ivy is a small glossy plant which is common along rivers in dry interior habitats. The poison is contained in an oil which on contact with the skin may cause redness, swelling, itchiness and blisters. These symptoms may even be caused by the smoke from a burned plant or by contact with clothing and shoes that have been contaminated by poison ivy. A friend of ours got blisters on his face from wiping his brow with contaminated hands in late summer along the Thompson River. Effective prevention is in learning to recognize, and then avoiding this green plant (scarlet in fall) with three-leaf clusters and whitish berries close to the stem. For known contact, wash the affected area and clothing immediately and thoroughly in several changes of soapy water. Apply zinc oxide lotion or calamine lotion for relief of pruritis.

Snake Bite

The northern Pacific rattler is the only poisonous snake in British Columbia and is found primarily in hot dry interior climates. Precautions to take in such areas in the summer are to avoid climbing around rocks without boots and never to reach for an unseen handhold on rocks. The bite of the rattler can be differentiated from that of non-poisonous snakes by the presence of puncture marks of the fangs on the outside end of the upper bite outline. Local symptoms caused by snake venom are severe pain, swelling and a purple discoloration of the skin. Systemic reaction to the venom results in general weakness, nausea, vomiting, rapid pulse, shortness of breath, and sometimes unconsciousness. However of the few snake bites that occur in British Columbia, deaths are very rare.

In case of a poisonous snake bite, act quickly to reassure the victim and to reduce the speed of blood circulation. Keep the patient as calm and still as possible. Where a limb is involved, constrict the area slightly by tying a one inch belt or piece of webbing between the bite and the heart. This constriction should be removed for about two minutes out of every twenty minutes. Cutting and sucking should be attempted where it can be done quickly and safely. A wound on the hand or foot where snake bites normally occur should not be opened up as there is too great a danger of severing vital blood vessels, nerves and tendons. But if the bite is in a muscular area, a sterilized knife or blade can be used to make a small incision 1/8 inch deep at each fang mark to create a blood flow. Suck out the poison, being careful not to swallow the poison if sucked by mouth. Suctioning is effective when it is done immediately but is of little use after a few minutes have elapsed. Put a cold pack around the affected area. Seek medical attention, phoning ahead where possible so that antivenom serum may be obtained.

Wasp and Bee Stings

Unless an individual has developed an allergy to wasp and bee stings, the symptoms are usually fairly local ones - pain and swelling. Treat by removing the stinger, if there is one, and applying cold. Zinc oxide or calamine lotion may relieve any itching. An antiallergenic medication should be given for any sign of systemic involvement such as rapid pulse, shortness of breath or extensive redness and swelling. Anyone with an allergy to insect stings should have medical advice and carry medication with them at all times during the wasp and bee season. Once a person has had an allergic reaction, subsequent bites are likely to cause increasingly severe reactions.

Tick Bites

Rocky Mountain or Paralysis Wood Ticks are prevalent in the spring and early summer in the dry grassland areas of British Columbia. They depend on blood for existence and attach themselves to passing mammals including man, from their position on grass and shrubs. To feed, the female tick attaches her mouth parts to the host by producing a quick-drying cement. Symptoms of paralysis develop only after the tick has been feeding for about five days, and begins with a numbness and gradual paralysis of the lower limbs, progressing to hands and arms and eventually to the throat muscles. It will result in death, unless the tick is removed, after which complete recovery follows. To avoid tick paralysis a daily examination of the body should be made, with special attention to hairline areas. To remove ticks, use tweezers and apply a slow, gentle pull.

Rocky Mountain spotted fever, another disease carried by ticks has not been known to occur from British Columbia ticks.

Another variety of tick, which may be encountered in wet vegetation along the coast is the Pacific coast tick. This tick does not cause paralysis but because of barbed mouth parts they are difficult to remove and the bite may develop into a slow healing ulcer. Strange removal techniques have been suggested including twisting the tick, applying an irritant such as turpentine to its backside or excising the mouth parts and then treating the wound with antiseptic.

OUTDOOR ETHICS

The outdoorsperson has a moral responsibility, not only to himself or herself but also to other people and to the environment. The following are a few points which relate to a canoeing experience:

— Divide large groups of canoeists into small parties for travelling and camping together, as this will make it easier for members of the group to keep track of one another, and will minimize congestion and environmental damage.
— Ask permission to land, cross, or camp on private property.
— For firewood use only the lower dead branches from large trees - do not damage live trees.
— Be aware of fire restrictions and be certain that fires are put out.
— Observe fishing and hunting regulations.
— Carry out all garbage that cannot be burned.

ROUTES

Following are the Canoe Routes divided into the area denoted on the map on page 2. An alphabetical index is on page 174.

All measurements have been given in the metric system. However since many people will still be using miles rather than kilometres, especially in driving distances, here are some formulas for changing from metric to the old English system:

Kilometres to miles = km x 0.621
Metres to feet = m x 3.281
Centimetres to inches = cm x 0.4
Hectares to acres = hectares x 2.471
Celsius to farenheit = c x 1.8 + 32

Note: Maps are intended for area reference only. The suggested topographic sheets should be purchased for the actual journey.

n/a indicates information not available at time of printing.

The designation Wild River, Natural River, Recreational River, and Scenic Shoreline noted by some of the routes are taken from a Draft Classification System for trails and rivers in B.C. prepared by the Outdoor Recreation Council of British Columbia. Their aim is to obtain legislation for some degree of protection to these rivers, an idea initiated by the B.C. Wildlife Federation several years ago.

Suggested criteria for this Draft Classification are as follows:

1. Wild River
— principal purpose is to preserve the wild and primitive qualities of the river
— generally inaccessible except by trail
— contains no impoundments, diversions, or other artificial modification of streamway
— of sufficient length to provide a wilderness experience
— high environmental quality

2. Natural River
— protected to maintain the natural appearance of the river environment
— road access is permitted insofar as it enhances public ability to enjoy the river and does not unduly detract from the natural values of the river
— must be free-flowing, although some minor alterations are permitted if they do not detract from the natural qualities of the river environment
— the overall environmental quality of the river should be high, with an emphasis on maintaining a natural appearing environment

3. Recreational River
— principal purpose is to provide, protect, and perpetuate opportunities for recreational activities associated with a river environment without degrading the natural or scenic qualities of the environment
— it is important that there exist good or potentially good public access

— river must be free flowing, although certain streamway modifications may be permitted that do not hinder recreational use
— Environmental quality should be good, maintaining the natural and scenic appearance as much as possible
— may exist near or even in an urban area

4. Scenic Shoreline
— ocean or lake shorelines that are protected to maintain scenic and natural qualities
— generally, these are to be areas of high public exposure as on a regular ferry route or the shoreline of a lake viewed or accessed by a major highway
— while no development is desirable on such shorelines, developments that do not detract, significantly from the scenic or natural values of the area are permitted
— environmental quality should be good

Recreationists who would like to contribute information or who would like to see a particular river, shoreline or trail given a certain status should send a trail or route report to the Outdoor Recreation Council of B.C., 1200 Hornby St., Vancouver, B.C. V6Z 1W2.

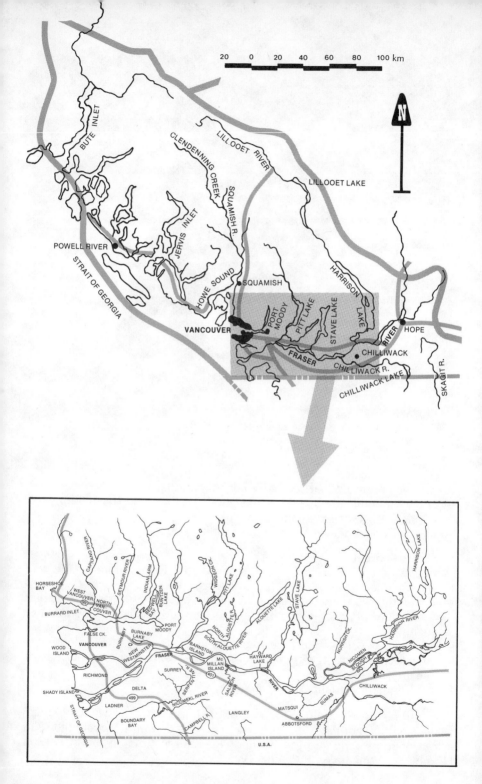

LOWER MAINLAND REGION

ROUTE - CAPILANO RIVER *Recreational River*
GRADE - *3 to 5*
LENGTH - *5.5 km*
WIDTH - *8 to 25 metres*
VERTICAL DROP - *76 metres, 14 metres per km*
TIME TO ALLOW - *2 to 4 hours*
NEAREST EMERGENCY COMMUNICATION - *Federal Fisheries Buildings at put-in, Park Royal at terminus*
CAMPING - ACCOMMODATION - *No camping*
MAPS - *B.C. Dept. of Lands and Forests, Special 5B south, Howe Sound Burrard Inlet, 1:31,680*
HAZARDS - *Grade 5 water, shallow*

DIRECTIONS

Follow Capilano road north to the foot of the Cleveland Dam, an area known as the Salmon Pools, where there is a small park. Put-in here and take-out at the river mouth, with access from Park Royal or Ambleside Beach. Check water levels before launching.

DESCRIPTION

This river is suitable only for closed boats and should not be attempted in open canoes. It is also recommended that all paddlers wear crash helmets and wet suits. A water gauge at the west end of the weir, near the salmon pools, indicates the difficulty of the water: 2 to 3 feet - easy; 4 to 6 feet - difficult; above 6 feet - expert only. The first time this is run paddlers should be accompanied by a local guide.

Every May 24th weekend there is a kayak race on the river that attracts international level paddlers, and provides a chance for spectators to watch various river maneuvers being run. It is a popular run due to the natural aspects of the shoreline which has been intruded on in only a few locations. Water levels are controlled by the dam and so are not always suitable for boating.

Do not attempt this river in an open canoe. Use a guide the first time down. Inexperienced paddlers have lost their lives on this river.

ROUTE - SEYMOUR RIVER *Recreational River*
GRADE - *2 to 3*
LENGTH - *3 km*
WIDTH - *30 metres*
VERTICAL DROP - *Approx. 7 metres*
TIME TO ALLOW - *1 hour or more*

NEAREST EMERGENCY COMMUNICATION - *Riverside homes and services, or North Vancouver.*

CAMPING - ACCOMMODATION - *Not appropriate*

MAPS - *B.C. Dept. of Lands and Forests, Special 5B south, Howe Sound Burrard Inlet, 1:31,680; or Vancouver Harbour nautical charts*

HAZARDS - *Rocks, and old weir at river mouth*

DIRECTIONS

The Seymour is accessible off the Dollarton Highway in North Vancouver, just east of the Dollarton Highway interchange on Highway 401. A side road here leads right, or south, to a short breakwater or dyke at the river mouth. Access higher on the river is restricted by private property.

DESCRIPTION:

This short stretch of river is most commonly used as a practice and training area for kayaks and canoes. It is ideal for novices learning whitewater. The river is rocky and usually shallow as there is a dam on the upper reaches. Near the lower bridge there is an old weir that creates a section of fast water and may be tricky for beginners, otherwise the run is fairly straightforward.

The river, like the nearby mountain and park, is named after Frederick Seymour, Governor of B.C. from 1864 to 1869.

The Seymour has a summer and winter run of steelhead, salmon in the summer and fall and a few coastal cutthroat near the mouth.

ROUTE - FALSE CREEK

GRADE - *Ocean*

LENGTH - *10 km*

WIDTH - *30 metres*

VERTICAL DROP - *Nil*

TIME TO ALLOW - *2 - 4 hours*

NEAREST EMERGENCY COMMUNICATION - *Almost any access point*

CAMPING - ACCOMMODATION - *Not appropriate*

MAPS - *City of Vancouver map or nautical chart*

HAZARDS - *Large boats and harbour traffic*

DIRECTIONS

Turn off Pacific to Sunset Beach launching ramp. Park here and launch, heading in an easterly direction.

DESCRIPTION

From the launching point head east under the Burrard Bridge and the Kitsilano railway trestle. Continue along the north shoreline and make a circle trip, returning along the south side. Along the way you will pass small industries, the Vancouver fireboat stationed at its seaside resort, the old C.P.R. yards, shipyards, and the new innovative housing complex. As well there are restaurants, marinas, bridges, mills and pedestrian walkways. Paddling this area can be an insight to the inner core of the city.

False Creek was named in the late 1850's by Captain Richards of the Royal Navy who sailed into the inlet thinking that it was the outlet of a stream. Finding the mudflats at the east end he notated that this was "False Creek." The east end has gradually been filled in so that the mud flats and drainage channels are no longer there.

ROUTE - SERPENTINE RIVER
GRADE - *1*
LENGTH - *16 km return*
WIDTH - *2 to 10 metres*
VERTICAL DROP - *6 metres*
TIME TO ALLOW - *1 day*
NEAREST EMERGENCY COMMUNICATION - *White Rock or Cloverdale*
CAMPING - ACCOMMODATION - *Not appropriate*
MAPS - *N.T.S. 1:50,000 92G/2 E&W New Westminster; Dominion Map Ltd., Fraser Valley*
HAZARDS - *Nil*

DIRECTIONS

Put-in and take-out at Highway 99A crossing, King George Highway. Paddle east to Highway 10, or portage beyond.

DESCRIPTION

This stream is similar except in the historic aspect to the Nickomekl. Distance given is to Highway 10 crossing, near Cloverdale. Paddlers wanting to travel further upstream would have to portage here. Canoes could be launched here and paddled downstream. Serpentine Fen bird refuge is at the western end of the journey and would be an interesting hike if time allows.

ROUTE - SALMON RIVER
GRADE - *1*
LENGTH - *10 km*
WIDTH - *1.5 to 5 metres*
VERTICAL DROP - *8 metres*
TIME TO ALLOW - *½ day*
NEAREST EMERGENCY COMMUNICATION - *Fort Langley*
CAMPING - ACCOMMODATION - *Fort Langley; no camping*
MAPS - *N.T.S. 1:50,000 92G/2E New Westminster*
HAZARDS - *Deadfall*

DIRECTIONS

Take the 401 freeway east to the 232nd St. exit. Follow #10 highway about 2 km to Glover Road. At this T junction turn right on Glover 1 km to McMillan Park. In highwater launch here. In low water continue north on Glover for 3 km to the Salmon River bridge, just south of Fort Langley. Launch here. Take out at Fort Langley.

DESCRIPTION

Canoeing the entire length of the salmon will be impractical and damaging to canoes, in anything except high water. With under two feet of water there will be a lot of deadfall and debris that will have to be run or carried over. Below the second launching site the river is considerably wider and deeper, and though close to Fort Langley, there is still 4 km of river to canoe.

It is more practical, using the lower launch site, to canoe the river, portage the flood gate to the Fraser, paddle the Fraser for 1.5 km and then walk the 1.5 km back to your vehicle at the bridge.

From McMillan Park, once the site of a Hudson's Bay Company Farm, the river flows slowly north, passing Trinity College and then going under the freeway in huge culverts. Except for the culverts this is the route taken by James McMillan in 1824 when he travelled up the Nicomekl River and down the Salmon to discover an appropriate site on the Fraser for Fort Langley.

Below the freeway there is a lot of willows and sloughed off banks which almost block the channel, then it opens a little and passes the Ziegler's Castle. This is private property so do not land. Then another set of culverts takes you under Rawlison Road and 1.5 km later the second launching point is reached. This area is popular for anglers.

Here the river makes a number of S bends, adding greatly to its length. Beaver and muskrat can sometimes be seen, as well as farm animals, and dead cars used to stabilize the banks. At the Fraser the dyke and flood gates will have to be portaged, and then there is a 1.5 km paddle to a pull out just upstream of the bridge to McMillan Island.

ROUTE - NICOMEKL RIVER *Recreational River*
GRADE - *1*
LENGTH - *20 km*
WIDTH - *1 to 10 metres*
VERTICAL DROP - *8 metres*
TIME TO ALLOW - *1 day*
NEAREST EMERGENCY COMMUNICATION - *Langley & White Rock*
CAMPING - ACCOMMODATION - *Not appropriate*
MAPS - *N.T.S. 1:50,000 92G/2 E&W New Westminster; Dominion Map Ltd., Fraser Valley*
HAZARDS - *Nil*

DIRECTIONS

Take Fraser Highway 1A to Langley. Put-in at Portage Park, south foot of 204th Street, or if water is low, at the bridge on 192nd Street, Latimer Road. Take-out at Highway 99A crossing or Crescent Beach. Alternative is to put-in at 99A and paddle upstream, returning to the same spot to take-out.

DESCRIPTION

The main appeal of this stream is the historic significance of it and the Salmon River in the discovery of the Fort Langley site. A sign in Portage Park explains. "From this point, December 1824, Chief Trader James McMillan and party, from Fort George, Hudson's Bay Company Columbia River Headquarters, portaged to the Salmon River, and on to the Fraser River, exploring its banks for a suitable site for a Fort to establish British occupation of the country by the Hudson's Bay Company. They located the mouth of the Fraser River."

It is probable that the Nikomekl had more water in it in 1824 than it does now, for the main problem in launching at Portage Park is finding enough water to float a canoe. During spring wet spells would probably be the best time, otherwise it will be necessary to keep checking lower down the river to find sufficient water. The main hazards, if they can be called such, are a few fallen trees, farm sewage, and locks at the mouth of the stream. The river winds through farm land, crossing under a total of nine bridges on its course to the sea. As well as farm stock you are likely to see great blue herons, chickadees, crows, waterfowl and songbirds. Once a good steelhead stream it is now poor fishing, although cutthroat, some salmon and Dolly Varden are found.

ROUTE - CAMPBELL RIVER
GRADE - *1*
LENGTH - *5 km*
WIDTH - *Few Metres*
VERTICAL DROP - *Nil*
TIME TO ALLOW - *3 hours*
NEAREST EMERGENCY COMMUNICATION - *White Rock*

CAMPING - ACCOMMODATION - *Not appropriate*
MAPS - *N.T.S. 1:126,720 92G/SE Langley*
HAZARDS - *None*

DIRECTIONS

Take 400 highway south to White Rock turn-off. The put-in is at the eastern end of White Rock, south of Marine Drive, near the baseball diamond in Semiamhoo Park. From here you may canoe upstream or downstream.

DESCRIPTION

Downstream 1 km is the Burlington Northern Railway trestle and the channel leading into Semiamhoo Bay, named for the Semiamu Indians, a word said to mean "half moon". Upstream 1.5 km the river enters a culvert and flows under the 400 highway. Though this is recommended as the turn around it is possible to canoe through the Peace Portal Golf Course, watching for flying golf balls, and continue a short distance upstream. The river soon narrows with frequent obstacles.

The Campbell River meanders through the Hazelmere Valley in South Surrey, emptying into the Pacific Ocean at Semiamhoo Bay. This lower section of the river is an interesting paddle for novice canoeists, though there can be some sweepers.

Gulls, kingfishers, great blue herons, and a variety of ducks may be seen as well as muskrats. Fishing is possible for salmon, cutthroat trout and steelhead.

The river level is severely affected by the tide so it is imperative that it be canoed at a medium to high tide.

ROUTE - McMILLAN ISLAND - FRASER RIVER
GRADE - *1*
LENGTH - *10 km round trip*
WIDTH - *100 to 400 metres*
VERTICAL DROP - *Negligible*
TIME TO ALLOW - *½ day*
NEAREST EMERGENCY COMMUNICATION - *Fort Langley*
CAMPING - ACCOMMODATION - *Accommodation at Fort Langley, camping not appropriate*
MAPS - *N.T.S. 1:50,000 92/2E New Westminster*
HAZARDS - *River traffic*

DIRECTIONS

Take the 401 Highway, or Albion Ferry from Haney, to Fort Langley. From Glover Road, the main street, turn east on Mavis for one block and then north on Church, across railway tracks to a small river side park with tables and toilets. Launch here.

DESCRIPTION

From the launch site it is best to paddle the slower current of Bedford Channel in an upstream easterly direction. At Endsleigh Point, the east end of the Island, turn left around McMillan Island into Russel Reach on the Fraser River. This is actually two Islands, McMillan, an Indian Reserve, and a small westernly section called Brae Island. The channel between the two is almost gone now so continue to Tavistock Point and make a left turn into Bedford Channel, back to your launch point.

The location of this trip provides canoeists with an interesting day combining some canoeing with a visit to fort Langley National Historic Park. The river routes offers a chance to see the life of the waterway from a different point of view. Tugs and fish boats pass by and in the channel gillnetters may be at work on their nets. It is a popular area for bar fishing while along the shore the tracks of small mammals may be seen.

Caution should be paid to tugs and other boats and log booms that may lie along shore. The current of the Fraser is deceptively strong so be sure to circumnavigate in a counter-clockwise direction, thereby paddling downstream on the Fraser.

If you arrived at Fort Langley via the 401 try returning on the free Albion ferry, taking the Lougheed highway back. You can rejoin the 401 just west of the Port Mann bridge.

ROUTE - BARNSTON ISLAND - FRASER RIVER
GRADE - *1*
LENGTH - *12 km round trip*
WIDTH - *200 to 400 metres*
VERTICAL DROP - *Negligible*
TIME TO ALLOW - *½ day*
NEAREST EMERGENCY COMMUNICATION - *Ferry terminals or island homes*
CAMPING - ACCOMMODATION - *Not appropriate*

35

MAPS - *N.T.S. 1:50,000 92G/2E New Westminster*
HAZARDS - *River traffic*

DIRECTIONS

Take the 401 east to 104th Avenue exit. Cross the freeway and follow 104th to its terminus at the Barnston Island ferry terminal, about 2.5 km. The boat launch and small parking area is to the left of the ferry loading ramp.

DESCRIPTION

This trip is similar to the paddle around McMillan Island. The launch point is in Parsons Channel and in order to avoid paddling upstream on the Fraser canoeists should head east, upstream from the launch point. At the east end of the island turn left around Mann Point into Bishops Reach in the Fraser. At the west end of the island Robert Point is rounded back into Parsons Channel.

The island is named after George Barnston, a Hudson's Bay Company clerk who was one of the party that founded Fort Langley in 1827. In 1847 he became a chief factor. The island was often under water until a dike was constructed, completly encircling what is now fine agricultural land. The dike is topped with a road that offers canoeists a chance to explore the island a little more while stretching leg muscles.

Be cautious of tugs, fish boats and log booms in the river.

ROUTE - WOOD ISLAND - FRASER RIVER
GRADE - *1*
LENGTH - *6 km return*
WIDTH - *35 metres*
VERTICAL DROP - *Nil*
TIME TO ALLOW - *½ day*
NEAREST EMERGENCY COMMUNICATION - *Richmond or nearby homes*
CAMPING - ACCOMMODATION - *Not appropriate*
MAPS - *N.T.S. 1:50,000 92G/3E Vancouver South*
HAZARDS - *River traffic, river current, some wind*

DIRECTIONS

To Richmond and then west on Sea Island Way. Take first right after crossing bridge over Fraser. North on Grauer Road and then west to McDonald Road. Turn right on McDonald toward the Fraser River, to a parking lot on the river's edge. Put in here and paddle toward the sea, west.

DESCRIPTION

This paddle along the Fraser River passes Wood Island and Iona Island, both excellent areas to view a variety of birdlife. This is an estuary environment, one abundant in small animal life. Herons may be seen feeding, owls hunting, and in the winter flocks of waterfowl and shorebirds such as dunlins, sandpipers, ducks and geese. As well there is the constant activity of the river: the tugs with barges and booms, the fishing boats and the freighters.

Be cautious of the fast flowing river. It will fluctuate with the tide and could be difficult paddling on the return journey. The water is not safe for drinking or swimming.

ROUTE - SHADY ISLAND - FRASER RIVER ESTUARY
GRADE - *Ocean and 1*
LENGTH - *6 km*
WIDTH - *1 km*
VERTICAL DROP - *Negligible*
TIME TO ALLOW - *2 hours to 1 day*
NEAREST EMERGENCY COMMUNICATION - *Steveston*
CAMPING - ACCOMMODATION - *Not appropriate*
MAPS - *N.T.S. 1:50,000 92G/4 Vancouver South; Dominion Map Ltd.*
HAZARDS - *River traffic*

DIRECTIONS

Take Highway 99 south to Steveston interchange, then west on Steveston Highway to Number 3 Road. Go south on number 3 to dyke. Put-in and take-out here. Paddle west along the shore.

DESCRIPTION

This short paddle along the shore of the Steveston area takes canoeists through a variety of river environments. There are log booms, tug boats, fish boats, canneries, a Japanese-Canadian settlement and a unique sand dune environment. There is a variety of shorebirds and waterfowl from nearby Reifel Island which in spring and fall is the stopping and feeding place of thousands of snowgeese. Watch out for river traffic and the wash of freighters against the shore, or booms.

ROUTE - PORT MOODY
GRADE - *Ocean*
LENGTH - *3 - 13 km*
WIDTH - *1 km*
VERTICAL DROP - *Nil*
TIME TO ALLOW - *2 hours to a day*
NEAREST EMERGENCY COMMUNICATION - *Port Moody*
CAMPING - ACCOMMODATION - *Not appropriate*
MAPS - *N.T.S. 1:50,000 92G/7W Coquitlam. Nautical charts of Vancouver Harbour*
HAZARDS - *Power Boats, ocean swells*

DIRECTIONS - Take the Barnet Highway through Port Moody to Ioco Road. Follow Ioco Road 2.5 km to Pleasantside Grocery Store, then turn left to Old Orchard Park. Launch here.

DESCRIPTION

Port Moody is the actual name of the east end of Burrard Inlet. Although at first glance it may appear somewhat too industrialized it can make a pleasant paddle for a day or evening as the city of Port Moody have retained all the waterfront from Old Orchard Park to Rocky Point.

A short paddle would start at Old Orchard, once the site of the Lion Lumber Company Mill, and head east along the shore line, exploring the ruins of old mill sites. Along the way a wide variety of birds can be seen, including great blue herons, cormorants, mallards, buffleheads, scoters, scaups, gulls, spotted sandpipers, chickadees, goldeneyes, wax wings, bandtailed pigeons and many more. Harbour seals sometimes come into the port after fish. At high tide the mudflats of Pigeon Cove will be covered enough to canoe close to shore, circling along the south side to Rocky Point. Be cautious of power boats launching at this point. A short paddle will take you across the inlet to your vehicle.

Longer trips can continue down the inlet, but it would be best to avoid the south shore because of the power boats, tugs and steamers. Reed Point Marina should be avoided likewise. Continue down the inlet past Carraholly Point and Landing to Burns Point light, the narrows, and then return along the north shore. This route will lead past the Burrard Thermal Plant, the Imperial Oil Refinery (hence Ioco) and the old Sunnyside Landing, back to your launching point.

Port Moody was named for Colonel Richard Clement Moody, the commanding officer of the Royal Engineers, stationed in B.C. from 1858-63. It was to have been the terminus of the C.P.R.

ROUTE - BEDWELL BAY - BALCARRA BAY
GRADE - *Ocean*
LENGTH - *6 km*
WIDTH - *Approx. 1 km*
VERTICAL DROP - *Nil*
TIME TO ALLOW - *½ to 1 day*
NEAREST EMERGENCY COMMUNICATION - *Port Moody*
CAMPING - ACCOMMODATION - *Not appropriate*
MAPS - *N.T.S. 1:50,000 92G/7W Coquitlam*
HAZARDS - *Power boats, ocean swells*

DIRECTIONS

Barnet Highway through Port Moody to Ioco Road. Follow Ioco Road to old townsite and turn right to Anmore Road. After 1 km turn left following signs to Bedwell Bay or Belcarra Park. Launch from Road leading to water on the right at Bedwell Bay, then drive your vehicle to the Belcarra Park parking lot. A short walk will take you back to your canoe, yet leave your vehicle easily located at the end of the circle trip.

DESCRIPTION

This circle route circumnavigates the penninsula of land that forms Bedwell Bay. Beginning in Bedwell you may notice a number of old mooring buoys, once used by the Royal Canadian Navy. Some wrecks are reported to lay on the bottom, 16 fathoms down. At the north end of the bay you will swing west, left, through or around Charles Reef to Jug Island in Indian Arm. Racoon Island lies one mile north, another destination for more ambitious paddlers. Down the west side of the penninsula, travelling south, the old Cosy Cove Landing is passed, and then a shoreline of rock wall to Coombe Landing. Whiskey Cove is next and then Hamber Island, which at high tide can be passed on the east side. At low tide, below 2.5 metres, the island is connected to the Turtle Head by a neck of land. South 0.5 km is Boulder Island. From the Turtle Head swing in to shore at Belcarra Park, the end of your paddle.

Along the length of your paddle a variety of birds such as cormorants, gulls and ducks, even eagles, may be seen. Sometimes harbour seals follow the flash of paddles.

Bedwell Bay was named for Edward P. Bedwell of the Royal Navy who was second master of the survey ship *Plumper* from 1857-60. Belcarra is said to come from two Gaelic words, "Bal" - the sun, and "Carra" - a lovely country. It was named in the 1870's and for many years this landing was a popular holiday and picnic spot, serviced by coastal steamers. Only recently was the road put in.

ROUTE - BUNTZEN LAKE
GRADE - *Lake*
LENGTH - *5 km*
WIDTH - *1 km*
VERTICAL DROP - *Nil*
TIME TO ALLOW - *2 hours to one day*
NEAREST EMERGENCY COMMUNICATION - *Telephone at end of Anmore Road; Police in Port Moody*
CAMPING - ACCOMMODATION - *No overnight camping at lake; Resort at end of Anmore Road*
MAPS - *N.T.S. 1:50,000 92G/7W Coquitlam*
HAZARDS - *Some snags, strong current near dam intake at north end of lake*

DIRECTIONS

Barnet Highway through Port Moody to Ioco Road Follow Ioco road to old townside and turn right to Anmore road. At the end of Anmore continue on gravel road 2 km to lake.

DESCRIPTION

Buntzen Lake is partially the result of a hydro-electric dam built at the north end, fed by Anmore Creek, Buntzen Creek and a tunnel which brings additional water from Coquitlam Lake, locked away in the watershed to the east. Originally called Trout Lake it is named for Johannes Buntzen, a Dane who was the first general manager of the old B.C. Electric Railway Company.

The major portion of the lake is 4 km long, lying north-south. A narrow channel connects this section to a small 1 km long section on which the power house tunnel and the penstocks are located. Eagle Mountain rises on the east side with several waterfalls tumbling into Buntzen Lake, a ridge on the west sepates the lake from Indian Arm. Hiking trails lead up both the ridge and Eagle Mountain, with paths at the north end leading down to Indian Arm.

This is a popular summer swimming area for people of the Coquitlam district. Motor boats are banned and some fish can be caught. Beware of strong currents at the north end around the penstocks.

ROUTE - BURNABY LAKE

GRADE - *Lake*
LENGTH - *4 km*
WIDTH - *400 metres*
VERTICAL DROP - *Nil*
TIME TO ALLOW - *½ day*
NEAREST EMERGENCY COMMUNICATION - *Burnaby Sports Pavilion*
CAMPING - ACCOMMODATION - *None*
MAPS - *N.T.S. 1:50,000 92G/2W New Westminster*
HAZARDS - *None*

DIRECTIONS

Take Sperling Avenue from either the Lougheed Highway or the 401 to Sproat Avenue. Turn east onto old Sperling, behind the Burnaby Swimming Pool, and go south 1 km to the Rowing circuit. A channel of the lake reaches the parking lot and canoes may be launched here.

DESCRIPTION

Burnaby Lake is a pleasant place to spend a few hours paddling and enjoying nature. It is suitable for novices and beginners. Basically the lake is almost a widening of Still Creek, or marshes surrounding the lake. As such it is choked with willows and aquatic growth in some areas, though much was cleared for the rowing circuit. This growth makes it ideal habitat for an abundance of birds and small wildlife. Canada geese nest here, and wood ducks and screech owls. On the north side of the lake is a nature house which would make an interesting visit and will help you understand the life of the lake.

Power boats are banned on the lake. Keep clear of the water control weir at the east exit of Still Creek.

The lake, from which the surrounding municipality takes its name, was named for Robert Burnaby, private secretary to Colonel Moody of the Royal Engineers.

ROUTE - PITT LAKE

GRADE - *Lake*
LENGTH - *30 km one way*
WIDTH - *1.5 to 4 km*
VERTICAL DROP - *Minimal*
TIME TO ALLOW - *2 - 3 days*
NEAREST EMERGENCY COMMUNICATION - *Haney 13 km south*
CAMPING - ACCOMMODATION - *Unorganized camping along lake shore*
MAPS - *N.T.S. 1:50,000 92G/7E Coquitlam; 92G/10E Pitt River*
HAZARDS - *Wind, tidal lake*

DIRECTIONS

Take the Lougheed or Barnet Highway to the Pitt River Bridge and at the east side turn left to Dewdney Trunk Road. The next intersection is a T, turn left on Harris. At McNeil turn right, following it around Sheridan Hill to Rannie or Neaves Road. Turn left and continue 6 km to the lake outlet. Launch here.

DESCRIPTION

Pitt Lake lies in a narrow valley of the Coast Mountains, fed and emptied by Pitt River. It is unique in that it is affected by the Pacific Ocean tide. This results in varying currents in the river and varying shorelines along the lake. Be sure to pull your canoe well up on shore. The Pitt River drains Garibaldi Provincial Park, and Golden Ears Provincial Park forms the west shoreline. Scenery is typical coastal mountains and rain forest.

Wildlife likely to be seen includes black bear, cougar, black tail deer and small mammals such as squirrels and so forth. Birds will include eagles and a variety of hawks, ducks, swans and shorebirds.

The lake is known as one severely affected by winds so paddlers should keep an eye on both the weather and the shoreline. The west shore is usually in the lee of any wind. Two small islands, Goose and Little Goose may provide an emergency shelter, and interesting exploring.

At the top end of the lake is the logging camp of Alvin, and several miles of road leading to timber licences. A water taxi provides access and the camp could be a source of emergency communication.

ROUTE - PITT POLDER
GRADE - *1*
LENGTH - *11 km +*
WIDTH - *5 to 100 metres*
VERTICAL DROP - *Nil*
TIME TO ALLOW - *2 hours to one day*
NEAREST EMERGENCY COMMUNICATION - *Haney 13 km south*
CAMPING - ACCOMMODATION - *None*
MAPS - *N.T.S. 1:50,000 92G/7E Coquitlam*
HAZARDS - *None*

DIRECTIONS

Follow directions to Pitt Lake launch site. Launch into open slough on right side of dike.

DESCRIPTION

The Polder offers many places to poke a canoe bow into, and the appeal is in discovering most of them yourself. However, one route to get you started is to launch into the Fish and Wildlife Management area on the right side of the river dike. When you launch there should be only one dike between you and the lake. Paddle across this slough, being careful to choose the deepest channels, heading for the mountain on the far side where it is joined by the southern dike. In this section you may see muskrat, herons, deer, hawks and carp in the shallow water.

In the far corner portage over the southern dike into the adjoining ditch. Paddle west to a large channel and then follow it south. This spreads out like the fingers of your hand, with one main stream heading toward the mountain side. Take your choice and watch for eagles, sandhill cranes, bittern, geese, beaver, deer, warblers, and few people. Do not disturb any nesting birds you might find. On your return turn left where the broad channel meets the dike you portaged over. This channel turns into a ditch which will lead you back to your car without the portage. It will take you a long time to explore all the polder.

The area was reclaimed from the river starting in 1929, the brainchild of Dr. Blom, an emigrant from Holland who realized the agricultural potential. Until then, and to a lesser degree since, it was a private duck shooting preserve. Now sections are part of the government green belt reserve. Over 2000 hectares were reclaimed with the aid of a complicated system of dikes and pumps. If you hike here obey all signs and close all gates.

ROUTE - WIDGEON CREEK *Recreational River*
GRADE - *1*
LENGTH - *10 km return*
WIDTH - *A few metres to 1 km*
VERTICAL DROP - *Minimal*
TIME TO ALLOW - *½ to one day*
NEAREST EMERGENCY COMMUNICATION - *Haney 13 km south*
CAMPING - ACCOMMODATION - *Some camping on Widgeon Creek*
MAPS - *N.T.S. 1:50,000 92G/7E Coquitlam*
HAZARDS - *Wind at launch area*

DIRECTIONS

Follow directions to Pitt Lake launch site. Cross the river to the west side. This is Widgeon Slough.

DESCRIPTION

Widgeon Creek is a small fast flowing creek that drops out of Widgeon Lake on the west side of Pitt Lake. When it reaches the valley bottom it enters or forms a delta, offering a myriad of channels and sloughs for a paddler to follow. The water is crystal clear and the swampy shoreline is ideal habitat for many birds and mammals. During migration hundreds of waterfowl use the area which has long been a favorite area for duck hunters.

Immediately after crossing Pitt Lake a large island is passed on the left, Siwash Island. This can be circled, but take care in the rivers current and do not attempt it on a windy day. Should a wind rise while you are in the slough the crossing of Pitt River can be difficult and dangerous.

This is a favorite area for school canoeing field trips and is heavily used by a canoe rental outlet, so don't be surprised if sunny spring days find it crowded. A 10 km trail follows up Widgeon Creek to the lake. The latter portion is quite steep. The area is named for the Widgeon ducks which frequent the area.

A Forest Service Recreational site, approachable only by water, is located at the height of navigation on Widgeon Creek. Here there is a picnic shelter, toilets, garbage containers, fireplaces and a camping area. Forest Service caution not to disturb nesting waterfowl.

ROUTE - ALOUETTE LAKE
GRADE - *Lake*
LENGTH - *18 km*
WIDTH - *100 to 1000 metres*
VERTICAL DROP - *Negligible*
TIME TO ALLOW - *1 day*
NEAREST EMERGENCY COMMUNICATION - *Golden Ears Provincial Park headquarters*
CAMPING - ACCOMMODATION - *Total of 351 campsites in park*
MAPS - *N.T.S. 1:50,000 92G/8W Stave Lake*
HAZARDS - *Wind, power boats, snags*

DIRECTIONS

Take Lougheed Highway 7 east to Haney. Follow local direction signs to Golden Ears Park. Put-in and take-out at south end of lake at boat ramp.

DESCRIPTION

Like Stave Lake, Alouette is part of a hydro electric project. Water from Alouette, dammed at the southern end, is tunnelled through a ridge to Stave Lake, about 40 metres lower in elevation. The west side of the lake borders Golden Ears Provincial Park, once part of Garibaldi Provincial Park. The name for the park comes from the peaks of Mount Blanshard, the dominant feature of this part of the Fraser Valley. In fall and winter the afternoon sun strikes the peaks and the snows reflect the pink and golden rays. It is said that this coloring of the peaks served as a sign to Indians that it was the time of salmon migrations.

In 1933 a disastrous fire swept through the Alouette Lake area, consuming more than 30 million board feet of timber. Today second growth covers the area, now being developed as a recreational area. The vegetation typifies the coastal region with heavy undergrowth, berry bushes and heavy timber. Black bear, black-tailed deer and cougar are the larger mammals seen.

About 5.5 km up the west side of the lake Gold Creek flows in and at the half way point the lake narrows for 1 km, then opens out into the north end. The Alouette River flows in at the north end. This was once called Lillooet Lake, later changed so as not to be confused with the larger lake of that name. Alouette may have been chosen because it sounds similar.

Canoeists must be cautious of the cold water, winds, power boats and snags that can make this a dangerous lake.

ROUTE - STAVE LAKE
GRADE - *Lake*
LENGTH - *30 km*
WIDTH - *1 - 2 km*
VERTICAL DROP - *Negligible*
TIME TO ALLOW - *1 - 3 days*
NEAREST EMERGENCY COMMUNICATION - *Ruskin or Mission city 18 km*
CAMPING - ACCOMMODATION - *Unorganized along lake or Rolley Lake Provincial Park, 2 km west of Stave Falls*
MAPS - *N.T.S. 1:50,000 92G/1W Sumas; 92G/8E&W Stave Lake*
HAZARDS - *Snags, wind, power boats.*

DIRECTIONS

Take Lougheed Highway 7 east to Ruskin and Wilson Road north to Dewdney Trunk and Stave Falls. Put-in off Burma Road, west side of lake. Take-out same place.

DESCRIPTION

At one time the shores and banks of Stave Lake and River provided the wood for a cooperage at Fort Langley. Now, instead of barrel staves, the lake provides hydro electric power. Dammed at its southern exit the lake is littered with deadheads and standing snags. These plus frequent winds and the use of the lake by power boats make it less than perfect for canoeing. However, it is still attractive.

The arm the dam is situated on is approximately 10 km long. Near the arm's exit into the main lake a creek flows in on the west side, from Sayres Lake. A short hike along the stream makes a good leg stretcher, and leads to the small but beautiful lake. The south end of the main arm is heavily festooned with snags, and subject to drawdown when water is low. Along the west side of the lake is a power house with electricity created by a tunnel from Alouette Lake. Stave River flows in at the north end.

Watch for various ducks, blacktail deer, black bear and smaller mammals such as squirrels. Vegetation is typical coast forest of Douglas fir, hemlock, western red cedar and balsam. Alder and cottonwood grow along the shores in places.

ROUTE - HAYWARD LAKE

GRADE - *Lake*
LENGTH - *400 metres*
VERTICAL DROP - *nil*
TIME TO ALLOW - *2 to 4 hours*
NEAREST EMERGENCY COMMUNICATION - *Stave Falls or Ruskin*
CAMPING - ACCOMMODATION - *Unorganized or at Rolley Lake Provincial Park, 2 km west of Stave Falls*
MAPS - *N.T.S. 1:50,000 92G/1W Sumas; Dominion Map Ltd., Fraser Valley*
HAZARDS - *Power house intake at south end, snags, log booms, some power boats*

DIRECTIONS

Lougheed Highway 7 east to Ruskin, then north to Stave Falls on the Dewdney Trunk Road. Put-in on west side. Take-out at south dam. Alternate put-in on left or east side at lower dam.

DESCRIPTION

This lake was once part of the Stave River and was created when the dam was built at Ruskin. There was little or no clearing done at the time of flooding and consequently the lake is dotted with snags and deadheads. B.C. Hydro owns the shoreline. Several creeks flow in, Steelhead, Hairsine and other, and the vegetation is typical coast forest. There are cutthroat and Dolly Varden that are best caught in spring and summer.

ROUTE - SOUTH ALOUETTE RIVER

GRADE - *1*
LENGTH - *6.5 km*
WIDTH - *10 to 25 metres*
VERTICAL DROP - *15 metres*
TIME TO ALLOW - *½ to one day*
NEAREST EMERGENCY COMMUNICATION - *Haney 2 miles south*
CAMPING - ACCOMMODATION - *Golden Ears Provincial Park*
MAPS - *N.T.S. 1:50,000 92G/2E New Westminster; 92/7E Coquitlam*
HAZARDS - *Sweepers and mini-rapids*

DIRECTIONS

See directions to North Alouette. Launch on 224th St. or 232nd in highwater; Neaves Road in low water. Take out at Neaves Road bridge.

DESCRIPTION

This trip is similar to the North Alouette, although through slightly more populated areas, Two vehicles are again best. The South branch is considerably wider than the North and sometimes will be too shallow for decent canoeing. A circle trip using both branches is described under the North Alouette.

ROUTE - NORTH ALOUETTE RIVER

GRADE - *1*
LENGTH - *8 km +*
WIDTH - *5 to 25 metres*
VERTICAL DROP - *15 metres*
TIME TO ALLOW - *½ to one day*
NEAREST EMERGENCY COMMUNICATION - *Haney 3 km south*
CAMPING - ACCOMMODATION - *Golden Ears Provincial Park on Alouette Lake*
MAPS - *N.T.S. 1:50,000 92G/2E New Westminster; 92G/7E Coquitlam*
HAZARDS - *Sweepers and mini-rapids*

DIRECTIONS

Take Lougheed highway east to Haney. At main junction traffic light, turn left, north, onto 224th St. At next light continue north, crossing the south Alouette after about 2 km. At 132nd St. the North Alouette is reached. Launch here, or if the water is high enough 1 km east on 132nd St. An alternate launching site for low water is at the take-out point at the Neaves Road bridge.

DESCRIPTION

This trip is best with two vehicles. One can be dropped at Neaves Road, reached via the Dewdney Trunk road off the Lougheed Highway, where it crosses the Alouette. For a longer paddle drop the vehicle at the South Alouette, Neaves Road crossing. Paddle down the North Alouette and up the lower section of the South to your vehicle. Another route, in high water, is to launch at the 232nd St. crossing of the North Alouette, canoe down it and then up the South Alouette to the 232nd St. crossing, less than a kilometre apart.

The North Alouette is an exciting interesting days paddle, starting with some fast shallow water that makes mini-rapids, graduating into a slow stream as it reaches the Pitt River. It is affected by the tide and the lower reaches may be slow going if the tide is rising. Should the tide be falling the river will be faster but back channels and ditches may not have sufficient water for exploring.

As the river begins to widen and slow you will notice a hill on the right with some nice spots to stop and rest. Near here drainage channels run in. One, to the north, provides access to Blaney Creek and a whole new area that can be paddled. Watch for places where a short portage will lead to another ditch or channel.

This area is like a mini-wilderness, with deer, coons, beaver, muskrat, eagles, hawks and a multitude of song birds often seen.

The normal take-out point is Neaves Road bridge, but the trip can be extended to include the South Alouette, or continued downstream to the Harris Road crossing. See Pitt Lake for Harris Road directions.

ROUTE - ALOUETTE-STAVE LAKE CIRCUIT

GRADE - *Lake to 1 +*

LENGTH - *Approx. 80 km, long portages*

WIDTH - *Varying*

VERTICAL DROP - *122 metres drop, then 122 metre climb*

TIME TO ALLOW - *2 to 4 days*

NEAREST EMERGENCY COMMUNICATION - *Haney, Ruskin, Port Hammond*

CAMPING - ACCOMMODATION - *Golden Ears Provincial Park and unorganized*

MAPS - *N.T.S. 1:50,000 92G/8W Stave Lake; 92G/1W Sumas; 92G/2E&W New Westminster; 92G/7E Coquitlam*

HAZARDS - *Wind on lakes, snags, power boats, river traffic*

DIRECTIONS

Put-in and take-out at Alouette Lake in Golden Ears Provincial Park.

DESCRIPTION

This route, recently pioneered and as yet travelled by only a very few, is an opportunity for Lower Mainland canoeists to experience some of the difficulties of an "expedition" type of trip without the expense of travelling far from home. It could be done on a weekend, or better yet a long weekend, and would be excellent training or breaking in for a longer more arduous trip in the wilderness. The journey, briefly detailed here, combines several of the previous route descriptions into one long return circuit.

Begin the journey on Alouette Lake, and paddle north 10 km to the diversion tunnel. Portage the ridge on the right. This is not a regular portage trail and will be accomplished only with a lot of effort and determination. There is a 305 metre climb up the ridge and then a similar drop, a total of about 1.5 km in length. Paddle south on Stave Lake 5 km and turn right into the southern arm. 6 km south is the first dam, best portaged on the right, about 1 km. Paddle south on Hayward Lake 3.5 km and portage 0.5 km on the left, keeping away from the water intake which is also on the left side. Follow a road south, or drop over the steep bank and put-in near the outlet from the generating station. The right side of the river is less swift and makes an easier passage. Beware of rising water from the dam.

Paddle south 3 km to the Fraser River at Ruskin and then west on the Fraser for 27 km. This is grade 1 water but the large volume can create tricky currents, eddies and boils. Turn right, upstream at the Pitt River. It would be easiest to paddle the Fraser on an outgoing tide, and then Pitt and Alouette Rivers on an incoming tide. Go up, north, on the Pitt for 5 km and then turn right into the Alouette. At the confluence of the North and South Alouette, take the right fork, the South branch. Remember this is now all upstream travel and the lower portions are affected by the tide. The distance you can paddle up the South Alouette will depend on the paddlers strength and the water level. It is 14 km from the Pitt River to Alouette Lake. Approximately half should be deep enough to paddle. This will bring you to about 232nd street, where it is possible to pull-out. The challenge of course is to complete the whole circuit, whether it takes paddling, lining, poling or portaging. There will be a final portage around the dam at the end of Alouette Lake, and then the 80 km is complete. This is not a trip for the faint-hearted but will be of interest to canoeists looking for something a little different in Lower Mainland canoeing.

See the descriptions of the Alouette Rivers, Alouette Lake, Stave Lake, Hayward Lake, Fraser River and Pitt River.

ROUTE - KANAKA CREEK *Recreational River*

GRADE - *1*

LENGTH - *12 km return*

WIDTH - *5 metres*

VERTICAL DROP - *25 metres*

TIME TO ALLOW - *2 hours to 1 day*

NEAREST EMERGENCY COMMUNICATION - *Haney 1 km west, on Highway 7*

CAMPING - ACCOMMODATIONS - *Golden Ears Provincial Park, 8 km north*

MAPS - *N.T.S. 1:250,000 92G2E New Westminster, Dominion Map Ltd., Fraser Valley*

HAZARDS - *Bridges, fallen trees*

DIRECTIONS

East on Highway 7, 1 km past Haney. Park on the south of the highway and paddle upstream. Take-out at same spot. Access is sometimes possible upstream, but is limited to private land, and permission must be obtained.

DESCRIPTION

This creek runs through an area designated for development as a regional park. Until the land status and park boundaries are settled and delineated the best access is off Highway 7. There is a large parking area east of the bridge and south of the highway.

The creek is named for the Kanakas, people from the Hawaiian Islands. By 1834 the Hudson's Bay Company had built a post at Honolulu, but even before that some of the Islanders had come to B.C. in trading ships.

Great blue herons, kingfishers, ducks, shorebirds and small mammals such as beaver are likely to be seen by canoeists. There are a few winter run steelhead still using the stream.

ROUTE - ROLLEY LAKE
GRADE - *Lake*
LENGTH - *1 km*
WIDTH - *0.5 km*
VERTICAL DROP - *Nil*
TIME TO ALLOW - *1 hour or more*
NEAREST EMERGENCY COMMUNICATION - *Rolley Lake Provincial Park headquarters*
CAMPING - ACCOMMODATION - *Rolley Lake Provincial Park*
MAPS - *N.T.S. 1:50,000 92G/1W Sumas; Dominion Map Ltd., Fraser Valley*
HAZARDS - *None*

DIRECTIONS

Approx. 2 km west of Stave Falls off Dewdney Trunk Road. Put-in at boat launch near picnic sites.

DESCRIPTION

The appeal of this small lake is not its size nor the diversity of plant life in the coastal forest but the fact that it is close to a provincial park campsite. There are 65 campsites here, as well as 28 picnic sites. This park could provide the base for exploring the canoeable streams and lakes of the Stave Lake area, and make a fine summer evenings canoeing. The lake is closed to power boats.

ROUTE - NICOMEN SLOUGH
GRADE - *Lake*
LENGTH - *Total lineal length canoeable - 32 km one way*
WIDTH - *10 to 40 metres*
VERTICAL DROP - *Nil*
TIME TO ALLOW - *2 hours to 1 day*
CAMPING - ACCOMMODATION - *Camping unorganized along Fraser dykes*
MAPS - *N.T.S. 1:50,000 92G/1E Sumas; Dominion Map, Fraser Valley*
HAZARDS - *Deadheads*

DIRECTIONS

Take Lougheed Highway 7 east to 1 km west of Deroche, at the highway bridge. Put-in and take out here. Roadside parking available.

DESCRIPTION

This large slough just 1½ hours east of Vancouver offers enough channels and shoreline to last at least a day, more likely two. Camping on the nearby Fraser dykes and river banks could provide an interesting, quiet weekend of canoeing. There are many possible access and egress points. If two vehicles are available it would be feasible to use Dewdney as one end

of the trip and Malcolm Road, 5 km east of Deroche, as the other. Putting in at the highway crossing divides the slough into two sections. The eastern part has 18 km of channels if you portage into Zaitscullachan and Malcolm slough, two interesting side channels. The western portion is more open and runs west 16 km to the Fraser River just down from Dewdney. This makes 32 km return.

Whatever route is chosen you are likely to see swans in fall and spring, Canada geese, great blue herons, buffleheads, scaups, coots, goldeneyes, mallards, chickadees, **gulls,** flickers and killdeer to name just a few. The dykes are lined with blackberries, elderberry, cedar, cottonwoods, equisetum, douglas maple, and hardhack. As well as dykes the eastern portion has some old beaver dams that have to be portaged, and in some places these furbearers may have returned. The grass and willow flats offer ideal grazing for birds such as swans and geese, and signs remind visitors not to molest the birds.

Fishing in the slough may bring in small cutthroat trout, steelhead, and coho. Trolling from a canoe is often most productive.

The slough is named for the island that borders the south side, an Indian word meaning near a big creek, ie Norrish Creek, on the north side near Dewdney. Dewdney is named for the Honorable Edgar Dewdney who with Walter Moberly built the trail also named for him. Deroche is named after Joseph Deroche the first settler of this area. He came from California in 1860.

ROUTE - HARRISON RIVER
GRADE - *1*
LENGTH - *18 km one way, plus 5 km for Morris Lake*
WIDTH - *Maximum 1.5 km*
VERTICAL DROP - *Negligible*
TIME TO ALLOW - *4 hours or more*
NEAREST EMERGENCY COMMUNICATION - *Harrison Hot Springs*
CAMPING - ACCOMMODATION - *Unorganized*
MAPS - *N.T.S. 1:50,000 92H/5W Harrison Lake*
HAZARDS - *Wind*

DIRECTIONS

Take 401 freeway east to Rosedale Agassiz bridge then west to Harrison Hot Springs; or Highway 7 to Harrison Hot Springs following north side of Fraser. Put-in at public beach in the town and take-out at the Highway 7 bridge. Two vehicles will be needed; or you can hitch-hike back.

DESCRIPTION

From the launching point paddle west along the shore of Harrison Lake, rounding Whippoorwill Point into Harrison River. The trip from here is an interesting one and can be lengthened as time and energy permits. The Harrison itself is wide and slow, almost lake grade rather than river, making it an ideal trip for a family.

A 5 km side trip can be made by turning right into Morris Creek and Lake, about half way through the river. The sloughs bordering this area are rich in birdlife, and a few mosquitoes. Seals are often seen following salmon into Harrison Lake, as well as deer and smaller mammals. The legendary Sasquatch, the hairy man of the mountains, has also been reported from the Morris-Chehalis area so keep a sharp eye out.

This trip is best made with two vehicles, but remember to take the keys with you and not leave them in the first vehicle. An alternative would be to hitchhike one way. Watch for wind on the broad river, particularly the lower end. Services are available in Harrison Hot Springs, though canoeists are advised to seek out the smaller restaurants. Canoeing attire is "inappropriate dress" for dining, or a coffee, at the main hotel.

ROUTE - HARRISON LAKE
GRADE - *Lake*
LENGTH - *Harrison Lake, 120 km return; Long Island 55 km return; Echo Island 32 km return*
WIDTH - *4 miles*
VERTICAL DROP - *Negligible*
TIME TO ALLOW - *1 day to one week*
NEAREST EMERGENCY COMMUNICATION - *Harrison Hot Springs*
CAMPING - ACCOMMODATION - *Unorganized*

MAPS - *N.T.S. 1:50,000 92H/5W; 92H/12W Mount Urquhart; 92G/9E Stave River*

HAZARDS - *High winds*

DIRECTIONS

Follow directions to Harrison River and put-in at public beach. Take-out at same place on return.

DESCRIPTION

There are several routes on this large lake which provide paddlers with routes of varying length, and as with most large lakes they can be altered to suit experience and time available. Canoeists must be aware that this lake is subject to high winds and storms. Paddlers should be strong and able to handle a boat in rough water and wind.

The first trip follows the route of early sternwheelers that carried miners to the goldfields trail, and covers the entire length of the lake, from Harrison Hot Springs to Port Douglas at the north end. This is 120 km return, a long paddle on a big lake. Anyone attempting it should carry sufficient supplies to last out a high wind or storm which could blow for several days.

Shorter trips, perhaps two days in length could go part way up the lake and return. One such paddle would be to circle Long Island, staying on the west side of the lake and circling to the east or right. Several small bays on the island could make interesting exploring. This is 55 km return.

A days paddle, though a long one, would circle Echo Island clockwise and enter Cascade Bay, returning down the east side of the lake. The return trip would be approximately 32 km.

On all these trips you must be prepared to stay out if a wind comes up. Try to stay close to shore.

Harrison Lake was named after Benjamin Harrison, a director, and during 1835-39, deputy governor of the Hudson's Bay Company. A Quaker, Harrison served without salary for fifty years as treasurer of Guy's Hospital in London. The hot springs which made the area popular were discovered by boaters who capsized during winter, and instead of freezing found themselves in warm water. If your canoe capsizes don't count on similar treatment.

ROUTE - SUMAS RIVER

GRADE - *Lake*

LENGTH - *32 km return*

WIDTH - *5 to 100 metres*

VERTICAL DROP - *Nil*

TIME TO ALLOW - *2 hours to one day*

NEAREST EMERGENCY COMMUNICATION - *Abbotsford or Freeway service stations*

CAMPING - ACCOMMODATION - *Cultus Lake*

MAPS - *N.T.S. 1:50,000 92G/1E Sumas*

HAZARDS - *Nil*

DIRECTIONS

Take 401 east from Vancouver to 16 km past Abbotsford. Take No. 3 road interchange, west 1 km to Jack MacDonald Park. Launch here.

DESCRIPTION

From this launching point it is possible to take trips in two directions, for a total of close to 32 return kilometres. Downstream, to the northeast, is the junction with the Vedder River and Fraser River. The Vedder is 5 km, with a portage over a small dam. The Fraser is approximately 0.5 km further. This route follows along the southeast side of Sumas Mountain.

The second trip takes an upstream journey, approximately 19 km return. This section is along the meander bends of the river, rather than the more channelized lower part. Another picnic site is located at Cole Road. There are a few cutthroat and salmon, and lots of blackberries.

This area was once a large, shallow, mosquito infested lake, stretching from Sumas to Vedder mountain. Many years ago the swampy waters were drained to provide agricultural land. Sumas is an Indian word meaning "a big level opening".

ROUTE - CHILLIWACK LAKE
GRADE - *Lake*
LENGTH - *22 km return*
WIDTH - *1.2 km*
VERTICAL DROP - *Nil*
TIME TO ALLOW - *2 hours to one day*
NEAREST EMERGENCY COMMUNICATION - *Vedder Crossing*
CAMPING - ACCOMMODATION - *Unorganized*
MAPS - *N.T.S. 1:50,000 92H/3W Skagit*
HAZARDS - *Wind and power boats*

DIRECTIONS

Take 401 to Vedder Road interchange. Follow Vedder Road to Chilliwack Lake Road and turn east, following the river to a parking lot at the south end of the lake. Launch here.

DESCRIPTION

Chilliwack Lake lies in a north south direction in the Skagit Range of the Coast Mountains. It is a mountain lake nestled below Paleface Mountain on the east and Lindeman on the west. As the west side is the most scenic it is best to paddle along that side, beneath rock bluffs and waterfalls. There is fishing in the lake for Dolly Varden, rainbow and cutthroat trout.

ROUTE - CHILLIWACK RIVER *Recreational River*
GRADE - *2, rapids to 5*
LENGTH - *20 km*

WIDTH - *20 to 100 metres*
VERTICAL DROP - *215 metres*
TIME TO ALLOW - *1 day*
NEAREST EMERGENCY COMMUNICATION - *Ponta Vista Cafe has phone, or Vedder Crossing.*
CAMPING - ACCOMMODATION - *Unorganized along river, or at Cultus Lake Provincial Park, south of Vedder Crossing.*
MAPS - *N.T.S. 1:50,000 92H/3W Skagit; 92H/4E&W Chilliwack*
HAZARDS - *Grade 5 rapids, cold water, log jams and floating logs.*

DIRECTIONS

Drive east on the 401 Highway to the Vedder Road interchange. Take Vedder Road south to Vedder Crossing and turn left, east, along the Chilliwack River Road. Follow the road and put-in at Foley Creek. Take-out at Vedder Crossing bridge.

DESCRIPTION

When the local Indians of the valley had been to the mouth of the Fraser for fishing or trading they would say that they were "going back up" the river, a phrase that sounded like the present Chilliwack. The tribe became known, naturally as the Chilliwacks, and the name was attached to the lake and river, and then a town.

Today it is certainly a down river run, and not one to be "going back up". Most of the river is suitable only for kayaks or closed canoes, although the 8 km stretch from Ponta Vista Cafe to the Vedder bridge can be run by open canoes. The valley is fairly heavily populated with summer homes and sub-divisions, but what has not been cleared is a typical coastal forest with heavy undergrowth. The high use results in little wildlife being seen.

The section of river from the lake to Foley Creek is used very little because of steep drops and log jams. The volume varies from a low of 340 cu.m/sec. to a high of 8500 cu.m/sec. The rivers depth ranges from 3 to 18 decimetres and the velocity from 5 to 16 km/h.

Foley Creek to Slesse Creek, the Chilliwack Canyon, is approximately 8 km in length with an average drop of 20 metres per km. This stretch is continuous whitewater through endless rock gardens, and is best run in low water, early spring or late summer. This stretch is for experts only in closed boats.

Slesse Creek to Tamihi rapids is about 10 km in length with a drop of 45 metres per km. Tamihi rapids are under the bridge 5 km upstream from the Ponta Vista Cafe. They reach grade 5 in high summer water. They must be portaged by open canoes, but the rest of the run can be taken by experts.
From Tamihi to Vedder Crossing is runnable by open canoes, but it will still be necessary to scout ahead and watch for all hazards. The drop in this section, which is about 11 km in length, is 4 metres per km.

The trip could be extended below Vedder Crossing, along the Vedder River.

ROUTE - SKAGIT RIVER *Natural River*
GRADE - *1 to 2*
LENGTH - *18 km*
WIDTH - *6 to 35 metres*
VERTICAL DROP - *Approx. 15 metres*
TIME TO ALLOW - *6 hours*
NEAREST EMERGENCY COMMUNICATION - *Hope 48 km south*
CAMPING - ACCOMMODATION - *45 sites along road*
MAPS - *N.T.S. 1:50,000 92H/3E Skagit*
HAZARDS - *Many log jams*

DIRECTIONS

Take 401 west to Silver Creek, approximately 145 km east of Vancouver, 3 km west of Hope. Turn south on Silver Creek Road for 48 km to the 25 mile Bridge crossing the Skagit. The put-in is on the left bank upstream of the bridge.

DESCRIPTION

THIS RIVER UNSAFE FOR CANOES. So reads the sign that greets paddlers about to start on a down river trip. And to a certain extent the sign is correct for the river is unsafe, unless paddled with caution, lots of scouting and by somewhat experienced canoeists. The main danger is log jams, lots of them. With careful scouting however, the dangers can be minimized. Other problems are the swiftness of the water and a few sweepers. These dangers combined can mean a slow trip with lots of work portaging and lining around obstacles. It is recommended as a group paddle, three canoes with one person having travelled the river before is ideal.

Almost everyone in B.C. if not Canada has heard of the Skagit River because of the controversy over the raising of the Ross Dam in Washington, an addition that would flood the valley from the launching point, downstream. Lost would be this unique, flat bottomed valley, so ideal for recreation and wildlife. A favorite stream for fly fishermen it contains ten to thirteen kilometers of the best spawning gravel on one of the few resident trout streams in the Lower Mainland. As well there is a deer herd numbering between 300 to 450 animals (intergrades between interior mule deer and coastal blacktail), black bear, cougar, beaver and other fur-bearers.

Every bend in the river offers a different view of mountains. Upstream is Silvertip Mountain, to the west Whitworth, and to the east rounded Shawatum, once the site of the town of Steamboat. Further south on the east side, actually in Manning Provincial Park, is Nepopekum Mountain and almost on the U.S.A. border, Hozameen, the site of an airplane crash many years ago. Across the border, high above the valley like an ancient castle stronghold is Mount Redoubt, seen to the west of Ross Lake. This is a river that should be paddled to remind us what can be lost for the sake of electricity.

ROUTE - SQUAMISH RIVER *Natural River*
GRADE - *1 to 2, some rapids could reach 4 in high water.*
LENGTH - *32 km*
WIDTH - *25 to 75 metres*
VERTICAL DROP - *30 metres*
TIME TO ALLOW - *6 hours*
NEAREST EMERGENCY COMMUNICATION - *Cheekye or Brackendale*
CAMPING - ACCOMMODATION - *Unorganized along route or Alice Lake Provincial Park, approximately 6 km east*
MAPS - *N.T.S. 1:50,000 92G/14E&W Cheakamus River*
HAZARDS - *Some deadheads, sweepers and small log jams, swift water.*

DIRECTIONS

Follow highway 99 north from Vancouver for 66 km, then a further 8 km to the **Cheekye** turn-off. From **Cheekye** turn left and follow the Squamish River 23 km north to a powerhouse. Put-in at the Powerhouse on the left side of the road after crossing the bridge. Take-out at Brackendale, left side of river.

DESCRIPTION

Canoeists using the Squamish should be sure to start at this Powerhouse put-in. Up river is suitable only for experienced kayakers in closed boats.

The Squamish is an excellent river on which to obtain river experience. The water is swift but most of the hazards such as log jams, sweepers and the small rapids, can be easily seen and avoided. Along the right or west side of the valley the snow-capped Tantalus Range is seen with beautiful scenes at each bend of the river. Bald eagles roost in the shoreline trees in large concentrations during salmon spawning and deer, bear and coyotes can be seen along the banks on occasion. You might even watch for moose as the Elaho River, the upper part of the Squamish, has a small resident herd which may gradually follow logging activity south.

The trip may also be started at Pillchuck Creek, a Chinook jargon word for red water. It may also be continued past Brackendale to a number of spots where the road comes close to the river, or even to Howe Sound and the Town of Squamish. Brackendale to Squamish is approximately 10 river kilometres.

ROUTE - LILLOOET RIVER - LILLOOET LAKE TO HARRISON LAKE
Natural River

GRADE - *2 to 3 with 6 rapids of grade 3 to 4*
LENGTH - *52 km*
WIDTH - *50 to 100 metres*
VERTICAL DROP - *180 metres*
TIME TO ALLOW - *2 to 3 days*
NEAREST EMERGENCY COMMUNICATION - *Pemberton, north; Harrison, south*
CAMPING - ACCOMMODATION - *Unorganized*
MAPS - *N.T.S. 1:250,000 92J Pemberton; 92G Vancouver*
HAZARDS - *Severe rapids, swift and cold water. Not suitable for open canoes. Canoeists are drowned almost every year.*

DIRECTIONS

From Pemberton drive south along Lillooet Lake to beginning of river. Alternate route is to come north from Harrison on rough logging road. Take out is at Port Douglas, or the bridge above, so one vehicle could be left here as a shuttle at journey's end.

DESCRIPTION

The Lillooet averages 1 to 4 metres in depth and flows 6 to 16 km/hr with a volume of 50 to 850 cu.m/sec.

This river is generally considered too swift and dangerous for canoes. It has been run successfully by groups of skilled kayakers and inflatables. Minimum raft or inflatable size is 3.5 metres. Headwalls, sharp right angle bends, leave little room for maneuvering and there are some sweepers. Be warned that many canoeists have tried this river and drowned.

The Lillooet runs through a deep valley flanked by 2800 metre snow capped peaks of Garibaldi Provincial Park on the west and the Lillooet range of the Coast Mountains on the east. Bears, deer, ducks frequent the valley, and reports indicate that Sasquatch also live here. The route follows that taken by early gold miners, though they stuck to a road for this part of the journey. The original route to the goldfields involved a steamer trip up Harrison Lake to Port Douglas, then a 55 metre walk or wagon trip to Lillooet Lake where another steamer was boarded to Port Pemberton. There wagons or shanks mare were used again to Anderson and Seton Lakes and finally the town of Lillooet.

The take-out point can be a bridge 8 km upstream from Harrison Lake, thereby missing one headwall rapid, or you can continue down to the logging camp, old Port Douglas. The logging road from here to the Chehalis or Harrison Mills is detailed in a series of books on backroads. Information may also be obtained from the Forest Service.

POWELL RIVER AREA - Detailed information was not available at the time of printing for this region but there is an excellent map available, published and designed by Gerhard Tollas of Powell River that shows a large number of canoeable lakes and road accesses. As well as lakes there are many inlets and bays in the ocean that are canoeable, some of which have portages to lakes or other inlets. With this map and some good topo sheets such as N.T.S. 1:250,00 92F Alberni; 92K Bute Inlet and 92G Vancouver, the canoeist should be able to keep paddling for weeks.

Remembering that this is coastal country and therefore likely to see a little rain now and them. Travel prepared with tarps and rain gear. And take your fishing gear for most of these lakes have excellent fishing.

The Powell River area is reached by taking the Langdale Ferry from Horseshoe Bay near Vancouver, travelling up the Sunshine coast and then taking another ferry to Saltery Bay from Earls Cove. If you are travelling with friends try to load two or more canoes on one vehicle to save on ferry fares.

QUEEN CHARLOTTE STRAIT

KNIGHT INLET

PORT
ALICE

NIMPKISH
LAKE

KELSEY
BAY

NIMPKISH RIVER

CAMPBELL RIVER

COURTENAY

STRAIT OF GEORGIA

MEGIN RIVER

PORT
ALBERNI

NANAIMO

LADYSMITH

DUNCAN

LAKE COWICHAN

COWICHAN R.

UCLUELET

NITINAT R.

NITINAT LAKE

BAMFIELD

CLO-OOSE

VICTORIA

N

20   0   20   40   60   80   100 km

VANCOUVER ISLAND REGION

ROUTE - COWICHAN LAKE
GRADE - *Lake*
LENGTH - *40 km*
WIDTH - *Up to 1.5 km*
VERTICAL DROP - *Nil, elevation 161 metres*
TIME TO ALLOW - *A few hours to 3 days*
NEAREST EMERGENCY COMMUNICATION- *Lake Cowichan or Duncan*
CAMPING - ACCOMMODATION - *Gordon Bay Provincial Park, south shore of lake, 30 km west of Duncan, 72 sites*
MAPS - *N.T.S. 1:50,000 92C16E&W*
HAZARDS - *Wind and power boats*

DIRECTIONS

From Duncan on Vancouver Island go west toward Lake Cowichan village. At the village swing up the south side of the lake to Gordon Bay Provincial Park. This is 30 km from Duncan. Launch and take-out here.

DESCRIPTION

This is one of the largest lakes on Vancouver Island. The south eastern end is separated into two long fingers, a better place for canoeing than the open waters of the larger part of the lake. The lake, named for a confederation of Indian tribes, was once called kaatza, which simply meant "the lake". Youbou, a village on the north side of the lake, is a compound name formed by two of the officers of the Empire Lumber Company in 1914, Yount, and Bouten.

For anglers the lake has rainbow, cutthroat and brown trout. The best fishing is from March to December, and not many canoeists will be out the rest of the year. Trolling or fly fishing is best.

There are several resorts on the lake which offer accommodation, camping, boat rentals, meals and supplies.

ROUTE - COWICHAN RIVER *Recreational River*
GRADE - *2 +, rapids to 4*
LENGTH - *32 km, 1 or more portages*
WIDTH - *10 to 25 metres*
VERTICAL DROP - *161 metres*
TIME TO ALLOW - *2 days*
NEAREST EMERGENCY COMMUNICATION - *Lake Cowichan or Duncan*
CAMPING - ACCOMMODATION - *Gordon Bay Provincial Park on Cowichan Lake, unorganized along route*
MAPS - *N.T.S. 1:50,000 92C/16E; 92B/13E&W*
HAZARDS - *Rapids, log jams, rapidly rising water*

DIRECTIONS

Go west from Duncan to Lake Cowichan. Put-in at Lakeview Park in the village. Take-out in Duncan.

DESCRIPTION

The Cowichan River was one of the first rivers to be proposed by the B.C. Wildlife Federation as a Recreational River, one of a system of Wild Rivers. The Federations aim was "not to restrict the area in its future growth, but rather, while that growth is taking place, to ensure that the recreational values of this river are not lost needlessly......to ensure that these values will be there for future generations to enjoy."

Not one to simply present briefs, the Cowichan Fish and Game Association began work on a project to construct a footpath along the river. This has come to be one of the most popular features of the river, and can be used by paddlers to scout out most of the river.

This is one of the best known recreational rivers on Vancouver Island. Steelhead trout, brown trout, rainbow and cutthroat all attract a large number of anglers. At various times there have been plans to channelize, dyke, dredge and/or dam parts of the river, but to date these plans have been so vigorously opposed by locals that they have not been completed. It is likely though that, like wilderness, the Cowichan will never be won forever, only lost forever.

This river is particularly popular with kayakers and being difficult for open canoes should only be attempted by expert paddlers. From the put-in point it is 10 km to Skutz Falls, which must be portaged. Five km Marie Canyon has three cascades that may be impassable and may require a portage. Check it out. Water levels will make a big difference. The 20 km to Duncan is easier, but there are spots that could prove tricky. Watch for log jams on the whole river.

Much of the land bordering the lower part of the river is private, causing a few access problems for paddlers. Check with land owners if you intend using other launch or take-out points.

ROUTE - QUENNELL LAKE
GRADE - *Lake*
LENGTH - *6 km*
WIDTH - *1 km*
VERTICAL DROP - *Nil*
TIME TO ALLOW - *2 hours to one day*
NEAREST EMERGENCY COMMUNICATION - *Lakeshore resorts or Nanaimo*
CAMPING - ACCOMMODATION - *At lake resorts*
MAPS - *N.T.S. 1:50,000 92G/4W Nanaimo*
HAZARDS - *None*

DIRECTIONS

Take the Island Highway south from Nanaimo approximately 5 km to Yellowpoint Road. Turn left, crossing the Nanaimo River after 2.5 km. Watch for a left turn shortly after onto another paved road. Eight km from the Island Highway make a right turn to the Zuiderzee Campsites. Launch here for a nominal fee. There is little or no public access to the lake.

DESCRIPTION

The length of this route is difficult to tally for although the lake is only about 2 km long it has about three arms, sort of a strange H shape. This makes the total straight line paddling about 6 km, but we were told that the shore line equals something like 32 km. At any rate it is not the length that makes this route interesting but the variety. Because of the shape there are lots of channels and backwaters to explore. Many birds use the lake as a resting and wintering area, including great blue herons, bald eagles, swans, loons, and various ducks and song birds. Deer are sometimes seen and mink, while around the campsites are an abundance of wild rabbits. There is fishing in the lake for trout and bass.

ROUTE - MEGIN RIVER
GRADE - *1 and lake*
LENGTH - *18 km*
WIDTH - *0.5 km*
VERTICAL DROP - *60 metres*
TIME TO ALLOW - *3 days to one week*
NEAREST EMERGENCY COMMUNICATION - *Tofino 50 km south*
CAMPING - ACCOMMODATION - *Unorganized*
MAPS - *N.T.S. 1:50,000 92E/8 Hesquiat*
HAZARDS - *Remote*

DIRECTIONS

Take Highway 4 to Tofino and then fly in to Megin Lake. An alternative is to paddle or take a boat 50 km up the coast to the river's mouth in Shelter Inlet.

DESCRIPTION

The remoteness and difficult access of this short river means that it receives little use, and therein lies its main appeal. It would be an ideal place for someone cruising the coast to put in for a few days and do some exploring by canoe.

From the coast you travel upstream 10 km, rising 50 metres to Megin Lake. The lake is about 4 km long and is fed by the Upper Megin. This is navigable for about 4.5 km, rising 50 metres in that distance.

Fishermen use the river, angling for coho and spring salmon, cutthroat and Dolly Varden trout in the deep river pools. Gravel beds in other sections of the river provide spawning beds. Eagles, black bear, mink and a variety of other bird and animal life are often seen along the river. The forest is typical rain forest of cedar, hemlock and spruce, with heavy undergrowth.

There are two shelters on the north side of Megin lake, near each end. This is a remote wilderness and paddlers must be familiar with survival techniques and wilderness travel before venturing on the journey.

ROUTE - NITINAT TRIANGLE *Scenic Shoreline*
GRADE - *Lake and 1 +*
LENGTH - *38 km, 4 or 5 portages*
WIDTH - *0.5 to 1 km*
VERTICAL DROP - *21 metres*
TIME TO ALLOW - *4 to 6 days*
NEAREST EMERGENCY COMMUNICATION - *Crown Zellerbach Camp on Nitinat Lake, Youbou on Cowichan Lake, and Lake Cowichan village*
CAMPING - ACCOMMODATION - *Unorganized*
MAPS - *N.T.S. 1:50,000 92C/15W&E Nitinat; 92C/10W&E Carmanah*
HAZARDS - *Wind, difficult portages, tidal surge, wilderness*

DIRECTIONS

From Duncan on the Island Highway drive west to Lake Cowichan. Take the north shore road through Youbou to Nitinat and turn left toward Cayuse. Before Cayuse turn right, following BCFS signs to Nitinat Lake. Launch at Knob Point Picnic Area.

DESCRIPTION

The Nitinat Triangle actually is a very diverse area for canoeing, and canoeists should not feel that the entire triangle of lakes and sea has to be travelled. In fact to do so would take an expert canoeist and wilderness traveller in good condition. However, portions of this route can be tackled to see the primitive endangered wilderness. The route described is a circle trip.

On Nitinat Lake it is a good idea to stay close to shore as winds come each morning, often with little warning. This lake empties into the sea and consequently has a wide variety of aquatic life ranging from salt water species near the ocean to fresh water species further up the lake. Canoeists are likely to see seals, otter, eagles, starfish, herons, kelp, gulls and other tidal creatures. Those not wanting to make the circuit could confine themselves to canoeing this lake, paying attention to the winds.

For the put-in, canoe down the lake, west along the right shore to the logged off Indian Reserve. There are two routes from here to Hobitan Lake. One involves wading and lining up the River, but this requires more water than is usually present. A portage trail lies approximately 1 km down the lake, to the west. It is 1.5 km long and is usually in good condition.

Hobitan Lake is approximately 7 km in length. It is good for fishing. Proceed west. If you wish to do some hiking canoe the left shore and watch for a trail that leads to Squalicum Lake. It begins at a small gravel beach at about the middle of Hobitan Lake. This trail is about 2 km long and although it can be used as a portage it climbs 70 metres so is a little steep.

Continuing the circuit requires a portage from Hobitan to Tsusiat. This trail is only partially cleared as a portage and requires some difficult carrying. A minimum of 1½ hours will be needed, with much more if it is during a heavy rain when the logs are slippery. It is not for the faint hearted.

To reach the sea from Tsusiat Lake requires wading down the river, but not too far. The river drops 20 metres into the sea. When you reach the bridge of the West Coast Trail leave the river and proceed down the trail to the Sauciat River at the mouth of Nitinat Lake.

There are two ways to make this trip much easier. One is to meet a party hiking the West Coast Trail itself, and give them your canoes while you hike the trail. Another is to have half your party canoe down Nitinat Lake, following the circuit in reverse, leaving their canoes at Whyac and taking the trail to meet you here.

It is possible to canoe down the coast if the water and weather are fine but there is a vicious tidal surge where the Sauciat River flows into the sea that will make it difficult to get into the lake. In reverse it would be a difficult run out to the sea. If the weather is foul the sea will be uncanoeable.

The seaward end of Nitinat Lake is one of the most interesting areas of the triangle for here the climax forest of fir, cedar and hemlock meets the sea life of the Pacific Ocean. This is one of the last valleys at sea level that is only partially logged. Where the lake narrows there is an old cannery, Whyac, and nearby is the old village of Clo-ose. This is a facinating place to spend a few days.

From here the circuit is completed by paddling back up the lake to the put-in point, at Knob Point.

Provincial Archives, B.C.

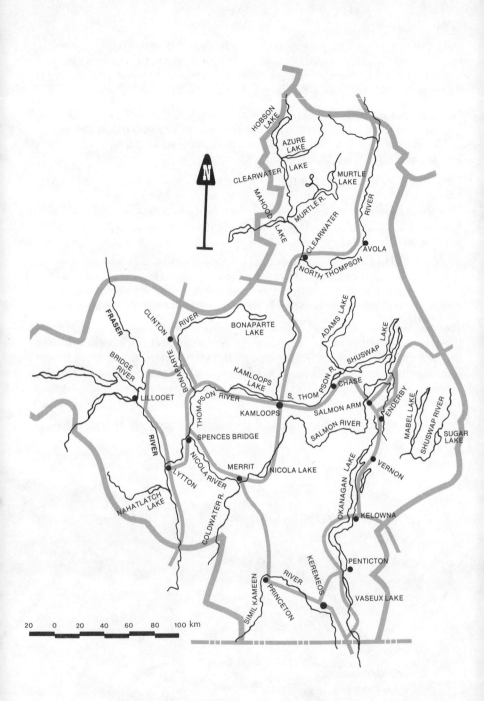

N

HOBSON LAKE

AZURE LAKE

CLEARWATER LAKE

MURTLE LAKE

MAHOOD LAKE

MURTLE R.

CLEARWATER

RIVER

AVOLA

NORTH THOMPSON

FRASER

CLINTON

BONAPARTE RIVER

BONAPARTE LAKE

ADAMS LAKE

SHUSWAP LAKE

BRIDGE RIVER

KAMLOOPS LAKE

S. THOMPSON R.

SHUSWAP R.

CHASE

LILLOOET

THOMPSON RIVER

KAMLOOPS

SALMON ARM

ENDERBY

MABEL LAKE

SHUSWAP RIVER

SUGAR LAKE

RIVER

SPENCES BRIDGE

SALMON RIVER

LYTTON

NICOLA RIVER

MERRIT

NICOLA LAKE

VERNON

NAHATLATCH LAKE

COLDWATER R.

OKANAGAN LAKE

KELOWNA

KEREMEOS

PENTICTON

SIMILKAMEEN

RIVER

PRINCETON

KEREMEOS

VASEUX LAKE

20 0 20 40 60 80 100 km

THOMPSON-OKANAGAN REGION

ROUTE - NAHATLATCH LAKES
GRADE - *Lake and 1*
LENGTH - *13 km*
WIDTH - *1 km*
VERTICAL DROP - *Minimal*
TIME TO ALLOW - *1 day and over*
NEAREST EMERGENCY COMMUNICATION - *North Bend 32 km*
CAMPING - ACCOMMODATION - *Unorganized*
MAPS - *N.T.S. 1:126,720 &3H/NW Yale; 92I/SW Lytton*
HAZARDS - *River below lowest lake must not be run, Grade 5 to 6*

DIRECTIONS

North on Trans-Canada to Boston Bar, then take the aerial car ferry to North Bend. Follow the Main road north to the Nahatlatch River crossing and turn left to a logging road that is often rough. Follow the road to the lakes.

DESCRIPTION

The Nahatlatch chain is comprised of four lakes connected with short streams, and is an easy paddle. Camping is possible on all the lakes, on beaches, but is best on the third lake, heading upstream. There is a major log jam above the fourth lake.

The Nahatlatch Needle rises above the north side of the last lake and the Two Squaws Mountain above the south side. The area has been logged but not enough to spoil the scenic qualities of the trip. Fishing is good for rainbow and Dolly Varden trout, and some steelhead, as well as being a salmon spawning area. Deer, bear and grouse are likely to be seen.

On no account attempt to run the river below the first or lowest lake. It has grade 5 and 6 rapids.

ROUTE - SIMILKAMEEN RIVER - PRINCETON TO U.S.A. BORDER
Recreational River
GRADE - *1 & 2 with rapids to 3*
LENGTH - *100 km*
WIDTH - *30 to 100 metres*
VERTICAL DROP - *274 metres*
TIME TO ALLOW - *2 to 4 days*
NEAREST EMERGENCY COMMUNICATION - *Princeton, Keremeos or Highway 3*
CAMPING - ACCOMMODATION - *Bromley Provincial Park, 19 km east of Princeton; Stemwinder Provincial Park, 39 km east of Princeton; unorganized along rest of route.*

MAPS - *N.T.S. 1:125,000 92H/SE Princeton; 82E/SW Penticton*
HAZARDS - *Rapids, gravel bars at low water, some snags*

DIRECTIONS

Take Highway 3 to Princeton. Drive through town to highway bridge crossing Similkameen. Put-in near Texaco station on right bank, downstream of bridge. Alternate put-in at campground 1.5 km downriver. Take-out at river crossing approximately 20 km downstream of Keremeos.

DESCRIPTION

Water levels in this river fluctuate radically, from a low of 170 cu.m/sec. in the fall, to 8500 cu.m/sec. in spring floods. This means that at times the river can only be run by experienced white water paddlers or rafters. Rescue procedures should be observed and known by all canoeists and more than two canoes should be in a party.

The Similkameen is a scenic river and makes a fine exciting paddle. It flows through the Dry Interior Zone, one of sage, ponderosa pine and a few riverbank deciduous trees such as cottonwood. For the whole route the river is flanked by the highway, and for some sections a dirt road follows the side opposite the highway. Wildlife likely to be seen includes deer and mountain goat in the vicinity of the Outward Bound Camp, where the Ashnola River flows in from the right.

From the launching point to Bromley Rock, about 19 km, the river is grade 1, sometimes grade 2. The rapids at Bromley can be grade 2 to 4, depending on water levels. Between there and Stemwinder campsite there are about 13 km of intermittent rapids to grade 3. From there to the end of the journey it is grade 2. All the rapids should be scouted as in high water there can be many souse holes ready to trap the unwary.

Near the point where the highway crosses the river a small canyon crowds the river, marking a spot where many years ago a group of American soldiers were ambushed and killed by Indians. Near Hedley the Great Corkscrew Road can be seen snaking its way to the Nickel Plate Mine where over 45 million dollars in gold was taken out between 1904 and 1955. Then the Chu-chu-a-waa Indian Reserve is passed and farther down the stream the old covered trestle of the Vancouver, Victoria and Eastern Railway & Navigation Co. This Great Northern subsidiary was run into the Hedley area during the gold boom of 1907-14. In 1916 an agreement was made with the Kettle Valley line to stop operations west of Princeton.

Many paddlers make Keremeos the end of the journey but the river is too pleasant a paddle to end here. Continue downstream past Cawston to the area where the river widens to form oxbows and islands. Just over half way from Cawston to the border a bridge crosses the river giving access to an Indian reserve on the west side. It is just below the remains of a covered railway trestle. This is an easy take-out. **There is a small picnic site** on the right bank and easy road access.

Alternate access is south another few km where the river forces the road against a rock bluff. Here an access road to farms could be used to

take-out, although permission should be sought from land owners. The river continues south across the border to Oroville, Washington, 22 km further, where it flows into the Okanagan river.

It is possible to begin the Similkameen journey upstream from Princeton, just below Similkameen Falls. The 45 km journey is grade 2 to 5 water and not suitable for open canoes. It is for kayaks only and is described by those having paddled it as passing through a continuous roaring chute and stair-case like rapids.

ROUTE - VASEUX LAKE
GRADE - *Lake*
LENGTH - *7 km*
WIDTH - *400 metres*
VERTICAL DROP - *Nil*
TIME TO ALLOW *1 hour to 1 day*
NEAREST EMERGENCY COMMUNICATION - *Okanagan Falls 2 km north*
CAMPING - ACCOMMODATION - *Vaseux Lake Provincial Park, 9 sites*
MAPS - *N.T.S. 1:125,000 82E/SW Penticton*
HAZARDS - *Nil*

DIRECTIONS

On Highway 97 29 km south of Penticton or 18 km north of Osoyoos.

DESCRIPTION

There are many lakes in the Okanagan valley that are of interest to the canoeist. Okanagan, Skaha, Osoyoos and others, but none have better canoeing water or points of interest than Vaseux. This is not a large lake, although the paddle may be extended by venturing into the river channels at either end. Bird life is abundant and for birders no lake could be better. Trumpeter swans, rest here in spring and fall, and geese nest here in summer. Coots, mallards, oriole, swallows, great horned owls, swifts, canyon wrens, ravens, magpies, Clarke's crows, hawks, meadow larks, and many more frequent the area. For wildlife photographers there are deer and California bighorn sheep in the hills above and both species often come to the lake shore.

The lake's name comes from the French word for muddy, probably referring to the amount of silt deposited. At the south end of the lake McIntyre bluff dominates the landscape, named for Peter McIntyre, one of the Overlanders that crossed Canada in 1862 in search of gold in the Cariboo.

Put-in and take-out at the Provincial Park campbround. Remember not to disturb any nesting birds that you might discover, and do not chase flightless, young, or molting adults.

ROUTE - SHUSWAP RIVER - SUGAR LAKE TO MABEL LAKE
GRADE - *n/a*
LENGTH - *Approx. 45 km*
WIDTH - *n/a*
VERTICAL DROP - *Approx. 200 metres*
TIME TO ALLOW - *1 to 2 days*
NEAREST EMERGENCY COMMUNICATION - *Cherryville and Lumby*
CAMPING - ACCOMMODATION - *Unorganized*
MAPS - *N.T.S. 1:126,720 82L/NE Revelstoke; 82L/SE Sugar Lake*
HAZARDS - *Route not detailed, grade 2 to 3 water estimated, many boulders*

DIRECTIONS

From Vernon head east on Highway 6 to Cherryville, then north along the Shuswap River to the dam at the outlet of Sugar Lake. Take out at Shuswap Falls dam.

DESCRIPTION

A detailed description of this route was not available but we include it for those who might want to scout it out and then canoe the whole Shuswap system. This upper section is suitable only for experienced canoeists during low water, ie the summer months. The route is bordered by roads on one or both sides all the way from Sugar to Mable Lake and should not be difficult to check out. Do not attempt this route without scouting or getting more information locally.

There is one grade 5 chute which will have to be portaged, below Cherryville, and not too far above Shuswap Falls. The falls are preceeded by a small lake. Pull out on the right as soon as this lake is entered. The dam is a weir structure and cannot be seen from canoes, much like a river ledge drop off. Portage on the right. Below the dam, log jams are reported so take care. Mabel Lake is described separately. Take-out anywhere on Mabel Lake.

ROUTE - MABEL LAKE
GRADE - *Lake*
LENGTH - *30 km*
WIDTH - *Approx. 1 km*
VERTICAL DROP - *Nil, Elevation 394 metres*
TIME TO ALLOW - *1 day*
NEAREST EMERGENCY COMMUNICATION - *Enderby and Mabel Lake Resort*
CAMPING - ACCOMMODATION - *Mabel Lake Provincial Park and Noisy Creek Public Use Area, Mabel Lake Resort has camping and accommodation*
MAPS - *N.T.S. 1:126,720 82L/NE Revelstoke*
HAZARDS - *Wind and power boats*

DIRECTIONS

From Enderby on Highway 97A take the Mabel Lake road east to public launch area at outlet of Shuswap River. From Vernon take Highway 6 east to Lumby, then north to the east side of the lake.

DESCRIPTION

Mabel Lake is part of the Shuswap River system and lies in the Monashee Mountains, east of the Okanagan Valley. A large lake, it is nestled in a deep valley scoured out centuries ago by glacial action. There are many interesting miles of shoreline for the canoeist to explore and enjoy, and many fine places to camp for a day or a week.

Fishing is good for rainbow, Dolly Varden and kokanee by trolling or on the fly. Near the Shuswap River outlet is Mabel Lake Resort which has boats for rent and fishing supplies, as well as campsites and accommodation.

Beaver, otter, mink, osprey, eagles, dippers, wood ducks, geese, a wide variety of songbirds, mule deer and black bear may all be seen along the lake's shore at various times, particularly by canoeists who paddle slowly and quietly.

A point of interest that canoeists may want to visit is a fine set of Indian pictographs. They are located up the lake from the Shuswap River outlet, on the west side, 400 metres south of the rock point at Tsuius Narrows. Blue penstemon grows here, and poison ivy, so take care when climbing or hiking.

The lake is subject to sudden strong winds and the water remains cold all year, facts which canoeists should pay caution to.

ROUTE - SHUSWAP RIVER - MABEL LAKE TO ENDERBY *Natural River*
GRADE - *1 to 2*
LENGTH - *40 km*
WIDTH - *10 to 50 metres*
VERTICAL DROP - *28 metres*
TIME TO ALLOW - *6 hours*
NEAREST EMERGENCY COMMUNICATION - *Hupel and Enderby; resort at Mabel Lake*
CAMPING - ACCOMMODATION - *Campgrounds on Mabel Lake*
MAPS - *N.T.S. 1:126,720 82L/NE Revelstoke; 82/NW Shuswap*
HAZARDS - *Cold water, snags, some rapids*

DIRECTIONS

From Enderby on 97A head east on the Mabel Lake Road to Mabel Lake. Best put-in is below Skookumchuck Rapids, 3 km from outlet of lake. Launching point is not clearly marked so watch for a cable crossing and launch below that point. Take-out at Enderby, at public launch site on left bank of river.

DESCRIPTION

This route is one of the finest in the Shuswap region, offering the whitewater of the Skookumchucks for kayakers and a fine, swift, interesting river for canoeists below that. Although not a beginners river it is suitable for novice river paddlers. The river is best travelled after high water has passed in late June or early July.

At one time this river was called the Spallumcheen River, and the South Thompson was known as the Shuswap. This is one of the strangest river routes in the province. A glance at a map will reveal the circuitous route taken from above Sugar Lake to Shuswap Lake, the river changing course over 180 degrees in some places. The river now takes its name from the Interor Salish tribe which inhabited the area when the fur traders first visited.

The river has no remarkable problems in the run to Enderby. Canoeists will have to pick a channel that is log free and deep enough at times, and a constant eye should be kept out for snags, but otherwise there should be no problems, Near 14 km is an area called the Islands, and so noted on most maps. This is a good area for some leisurely exploring.

Take-out points include the Ashton Creek bridge at approximately 25 km. The end of the paddle is a boat launching ramp and marina on the left side of the river just over 1 km downstream from the crossing of Highway 97A. . The trip can be continued another 32 km to Mara Lake. This route is also described in this book.

ROUTE - SHUSWAP RIVER - ENDERBY TO MARA LAKE *Recreational River*
GRADE - *1*
LENGTH - *32 km*
WIDTH - *10 to 50 metres*
VERTICAL DROP - *17 metres*
TIME TO ALLOW - *1 to 2 days*
NEAREST EMERGENCY COMMUNICATION - *Enderby, Grindrod, Mara Lake*
CAMPING - ACCOMMODATION - *Private land along river so ask permission. Picnic site at Grindrod and campground at Mara Provincial Park*
MAPS - *N.T.S. 1:126,720 82L/NW Shuswap*
HAZARDS - *Deadheads, snags, some power boats*

DIRECTIONS

Put-in at Enderby launching site, downstream of highway 97A crossing. Take-out at Mara Provincial Park.

DESCRIPTION

The Shuswap River is not one of the longest in this guide but it has been divided into three sections as each seems suitable for different paddling experience. This final segment to Mara Lake is grade 1, and suitable for beginner river paddlers.

Wildlife is much the same as the upper portions of the river with a wide variety of waterfowl and aquatic life. Large mammals are not quite so common in this agricultural area though. The river between Enderby and Mara Lake is a series of large bends and oxbows. As the crow flies it is only 20 km to Mara Lake, but by river 32.

This valley was one of the first to be settled in the province and the number of old homesteads along the route are evidence of this. Some of the Overlanders of 1862 came here at the end of their Thompson River trip, and either stayed or returned later to build the communities now in existence. Mara, Fortune, McQueen, McIntyre all stayed in the Shuswap or Okanagan valleys.

Take-out for this portion of the river is at Mara Provincial Park on the east or right bank of Mara Lake. There are 26 picnic units here with a changehouse and boat launching ramp.

ROUTE - CLEARWATER - AZURE LAKES - WELLS GRAY PARK

GRADE - *Lake and grade 1*
LENGTH - *103 km return*
WIDTH - *100 metres to 1 km*
VERTICAL DROP - *Negligible*
TIME TO ALLOW - *4 days to one week*
NEAREST EMERGENCY COMMUNICATION - *Ranger station at Clearwater Lake, Helmcken Falls Lodge and Clearwater.*
CAMPING - ACCOMMODATION - *Accommodation in Clearwater or at Helmcken Falls Lodge. Camping in Park at Dawson Falls and Clearwater Lake. Unorganized on lakes*
MAPS - *N.T.S. 1:250,000 93A Quesnel Lake; 83D-C Canoe River*
HAZARDS - *Wind on Azure, fast water between lakes*

DIRECTIONS

Drive north from Kamloops 122 km to Clearwater on the Yellowhead Highway. Clearwater Lake is 72 km north.

DESCRIPTION

Wells Gray Provincial Park is one of the largest wilderness reserves in the province, a region of extinct volcanoes, wild rivers, towering waterfalls, extensive icefields and unclimbed mountains. The park's remote corners have only been visited by a handful of men and its waterways were only discovered this century. Helmcken Falls, which attracts more people to the park than any other single feature, was only found in 1913. They are named after Dr. John Sebastian Helmcken, a pioneer doctor of the Victoria area and a member of B.C.'s first legislative assembly.

Unfortunately the region's rivers have attracted too much attention. As early as 1918 the *Kamloops Sentinel* stated that the "wonderful water power" was "still unused." An article said that "if 50 miles closer it would easily solve the hydro-electric question for the city of Kamloops."

More recently the Fraser River Board report of 1963, recently revived, suggests three dams in the park for flood control and power. Such dams would mean the end of the Clearwater River, one of the most interesting and beautiful in the province.

Canoeists heading to Wells Gray for the first time will probably take the route up Clearwater and Azure Lakes. It is certainly one of the finest. Clearwater Lake is 26 km long, emptying out the south end over Osprey Falls into the Clearwater River. At the north end it receives the flows of the Clearwater River from Hobson Lake, and the Azure River from Azure Lake. All boats must turn into Azure. The Clearwater River to Hobson is impassable for any type of craft, kayaks, rafts and riverboats included. In 1971 three kayakers tried the run and all three were killed.

The river connecting Clearwater and Azure is swift and difficult to paddle upstream, although at low water strong paddlers can make it. An easier route is to paddle up the river a short distance and then take the portage on the left which leads into Azure Lake. It is approximately 1.5 km in length, and unfortunately leads through a small marsh. Those attempting the upstream paddle would be best to stay on the right side of the river (facing downstream it is the right) and proceed upstream of where the Azure flows in. Cross the Clearwater and sneak behind an island that lies on the left bank of the Clearwater and the right bank of the Azure.

Azure lake is also approximately 26 km long. Lying east-west it is very susceptible to high winds and canoeists caught at the eastern end may be storm bound for a few hours or a couple of days. Campsites are easy to find. There is a bay on the south shore near the west end, the mouth of Garnet Creek on the north, and a small developed site near Rainbow Falls, on the south side at the east end.

The return journey is easy and most novice paddlers will be able to run the river. Watch for a tricky current where the two rivers join. There are lots of good camping places on Clearwater Lake, including some with beaches. Parks Branch brochure maps show most of them.

Watch for eagles and osprey on both lakes, black bears, caribou, moose, beaver, otter, mink, beaver, pika and waterfowl such as scoters, mallards, mergansers, and some geese are seen on most park waters. The south end of Clearwater is a particularly good place to watch.

Do not paddle to the south end of Clearwater Lake as the water flows out over a waterfall created by a lava dam that has formed the lake. Many people have drowned at these falls. Keep well away.

ROUTE - MURTLE LAKE - WELLS GRAY PARK
GRADE - *Lake*
LENGTH - *North arm, 21 km; West arm, 19 km*
WIDTH - *0.5 km to 5 km*
VERTICAL DROP - *Nil, Elevation 1067 metres*
TIME TO ALLOW - *3 days to 2 weeks*
NEAREST EMERGENCY COMMUNICATION - *Blue River; There is a ranger station on Murtle Lake*
CAMPING - ACCOMMODATION - *Unorganized*
MAPS - *N.T.S. 1:250,000 83D Canoe River*
HAZARDS - *Wind, remote*

DIRECTIONS

From Blue River on Highway 5 proceed west on a gravel road. A 2 km portage is necessary from the end of the road to Murtle Lagoon.

DESCRIPTION

Murtle Lake is situated in Wells Gray Provincial Park, within the Murtle Lake Nature Conservancy. This means that no motors - boat, car, or plane - are allowed in the area, hence the road does not reach the lake. For canoeists this means that they will not be bothered by the noise of outboards, or for that matter by planes landing. This is wilderness, a conservancy that will remain wild. Any paddler will be doing well to see the lake in a few days, or even a few weeks. It is very large and has a variety of trails leading to interesting volcanic features or other lakes. At the outlet end there is a 40 km trail that leads to the park entrance on the Clearwater valley side. There are trails to McDougall Lake, Anderson Lake and the Kostal Cone.

Fishing is good for medium sized rainbow on the fly, by spinning or trolling. The outlet of the lake is excellent, but a little dangerous for canoes. Do not attempt to run the Murtle River. There are several waterfalls along its course. Eagles and osprey both nest at the outlet end of the west arm and moose, bear, caribou, wolves and many small mammals are often seen.

To say too much about this magnificent country would only take the edge off a paddlers exploration. This is wilderness canoe country, enjoy it.

ROUTE - MAHOOD LAKE - WELLS GRAY PARK
GRADE - *Lake*
LENGTH - *21 km*
WIDTH - *1.5 km*
VERTICAL DROP - *Nil, Elevation 627 metres*
TIME TO ALLOW - *1 to 3 days*
NEAREST EMERGENCY COMMUNICATION - *Park headquarters or 100 Mile House*
CAMPING - ACCOMMODATION - *Campground at west end of lake, primitive sites on lake.*
MAPS - *N.T.S. 1:50,000 92P/16 Mahood Lake; 92P15 Canim Lake*
HAZARDS - *None*

DIRECTIONS

From Highway 24 head north to Canim, and Mahood Lake. Put-in and take-out at lakeshore launching ramp.

DESCRIPTION

Although part of Wells Gray Provincial Park this lake is not approachable from the North Thompson side. You must take Highway 24 and then 90 north through the Bridge Lake country to Mahood. The lake is a popular one with fishermen, and canoeists will have to put up with power boats on this lake. There are lake trout, rainbow, whitefish and kokanee in Mahood. Trolling produces the most fish but flyfishing is good at the outlet of the lake into the Mahood River.

Mahood Lake was named after James Adam Mahood, land surveyor, who died in 1901. He conducted a C.P.R. survey party along the shore of the lake in 1872 and the name appears on a map of 1883.

ROUTE - NORTH THOMPSON RIVER - AVOLA TO CLEARWATER

Recreational River

GRADE - *2 to 3 with some 4, 1 portage*

LENGTH - *72 km*

WIDTH - *30 to 60 metres*

VERTICAL DROP - *Approximately 175 metres*

TIME TO ALLOW - *2 days*

NEAREST EMERGENCY COMMUNICATION - *R.C.M.P. at Blue River, Clearwater and Kamloops. Phone at Avola, Vavenby, Birch Island and Clearwater.*

CAMPING - ACCOMMODATION - *Accommodation at Avola and Clearwater. North Thompson River Provincial Park at Clearwater, 63 campsites on river. Unorganized along route*

MAPS - *N.T.S. 1:250,000 82M Seymour Arm; 92P Bonaparte Lake*

HAZARDS - *Snags, deadheads, rapids*

DIRECTIONS

Take Highway 5 north from Kamloops 190 km to Avola. Launch at Highway crossing or upstream a few km. Take-out at Clearwater bridge.

DESCRIPTION

This section of the North Thompson is for intermediate paddlers only. Novices should start at Clearwater which is described in the next section. The river is graded 2 to 3 with some grade 4 and some sections will require considerable skill to successfully maneuver through the rapids. A minimum of three canoes should be used.

The North Thompson River has its headwaters on the east slope of the Cariboo Mountains. On the other side of the mountain divide, the Clearwater begins in Wells Gray Park. This section of the river is in the Subalpine Forest biotic zone where spruce dominates the landscape. Around Avola a section of the Interior wet belt is traversed and cedar becomes common. Further south again, near Kamloops the river passes into the Dry Interior zone.

From its headwaters the North Thompson picks up the flow of the Albreda River, Thunder River and Blue River, as well as numerous creeks. Just above Avola the river crashes and forces its way through Porte d'Enfer Canyon, a constriction much like Hell's Gate on the Fraser. Then the river widens and slows into Cottonwood Flats and Stillwater Flats, the latter now called Avola and the beginning of the canoe trip down the river.

From the launch point there is calm, flat water for about 5 km, when the water increases to grade 2. This lasts until Wire Cache, marked by the remains of an old logging bridge. Wire Cache was named when F.J. Barnard stored wire here in 1875 while working on a Dominion Government contract to run a telegraph up the North Thompson Valley. From here the water is 2+, with Raceturn Rapids just a kilometre downstream. The fast water then continues to Mad River Canyon.

Canoeists must take out here. There are warning signs placed by the Kamloops Canoe and Kayak Club. The signs are black on fluoresent red, and show a canoe with a large X over it. There is grade 4 water around the corner. In 60 metres the river drops 3 metres. Another short section of rough water occurs just below the canyon where the Mad River flows in. Portage up the right bank to Highway 5. Go down the highway to about 1 km to the south side of Mad River and put-in again.

The Thompson River Overlander party had a few problems here and must have found these rapids rather discouraging. They had to abandon their rafts at Porte d'Enfer Canyon and rebuild on the down river side. Now they ran into this rough water and swamped. Fortunately no lives were lost here but some of the men decided to walk from this point, no longer trusting the waters of the Thompson.

From Mad River Rapids to Vavenby grade 3 water can be expected in some places. From there the river is slightly easier, grade 2 to 3, though snags and sweepers must be watched for. This is a good wildlife area and beaver, otter, and deer may be seen. Canada geese also nest around Vavenby and Ospreys are often seen. More historical and natural history detail of this area can be found in *Yellowhead Mileposts Vol. 1,* by the authors of this book and published by Mitchell Press.

Birch Island is passed below Vavenby and it could be a pleasant stop for canoeists who want to visit an old general store. McCracken's General Store has been operated by the same family for more than half a century and has changed little in that time. Clearwater is just a few kilometres downstream, just below Raft River, the site of spawning salmon in the fall. Take-out at the trestle bridge in Clearwater, or continue down to Kamloops, another 130 km.

Canoes for this trip may be rented from Interior Canoe Outfitters in Kamloops. They warn that the Avola to Vavenby section should be avoided in highwater due to cold water and fast current, and a large number of trees in the river due to bank erosion. This section is best in the fall.

ROUTE - NORTH THOMPSON RIVER - CLEARWATER TO KAMLOOPS
Recreational River
GRADE - *1 to 2 +*
LENGTH - *130 km*
WIDTH - *50 to 150 metres*
VERTICAL DROP - *65 metres*
TIME TO ALLOW - *2 to 3 days*
NEAREST EMERGENCY COMMUNICATION - *Clearwater, Little Fort, Barriere, Louis Creek, McLure Ferry, Heffley Creek and Kamloops*
CAMPING - ACCOMMODATION - *North Thompson River Provincial Park at Clearwater, and unorganized along rest of route.*
MAPS - *N.T.S. 1:250,000 92P Bonaparte River; 92I Ashcroft*
HAZARDS - *Snags, some rocks, gravel and sand bars*

DIRECTIONS

Drive north on Highway 5 from Kamloops to Clearwater, 122 km. Put-in at townsite, where trestle bridge crosses the river. Take-out at Kamloops.

DESCRIPTION

This lower section of the North Thompson is much more suitable for novice paddlers and it is for that reason that it is afforded a separate description. The average canoeist with river experience, or with considerable lake paddling experience can handle this trip. Care should be taken to watch for snags, and some high winds may blow on the long open stretches. Novices should scout any areas that appear tricky and in particular Fishtrap Canyon. A minimum of two canoes should be used on this trip.

From Clearwater the river is an easy grade 2 to Barriere. Here the water speeds up and enters Fishtrap Rapids or Canyon 15 km downstream. Then there is a calm section again for 20 km. Above Heffley Creek watch for a quick transition from calm water to turbulent water at the junction of Jamison Creek, where 3 km of rough water will be encountered. These are known as the Heffley Rapids and are rated at 2 +. From there it is 25 km to Kamloops with no particular problems.

Canoes for this trip may be rented, and more information may be obtained from Interior Canoe Outfitters in Kamloops.

ROUTE - SOUTH THOMPSON RIVER - CHASE TO KAMLOOPS
Recreational River
GRADE - *1*
LENGTH - *58 km*
WIDTH - *15 to 30 metres*
VERTICAL DROP - *Minimal*
TIME TO ALLOW - *1 to 2 days*
NEAREST EMERGENCY COMMUNICATION - *Chase or Kamloops; Trans-Canada Highway parallels river most of the way.*
CAMPING - ACCOMMODATION - *Accommodation in Chase or Kamloops. Camping unorganized. Ask permission on private lands*
MAPS - *N.T.S. 1:126,720 82I/NW Shuswap Lake; 92I/NE Kamloops Lake*
HAZARDS - *Some power boats*

DIRECTIONS

Take the Trans-Canada Highway east from Kamloops to Chase, approximately 50 km. At Chase put-in from public access road, just west of road to the bridge over the Thompson. Take-out in Kamloops, at Riverside Park, located on the left bank.

DESCRIPTION

This river is one that can easily be paddled either way, upstream or downstream. Naturally however, the downstream journey will be easier.

The trip leads through areas that are developed in one way or another, everything from semi-wild through agricultural land to housing developments. Access to the river is generally poor. The river runs through the Interior Dry Belt and along the banks cactus, sage brush, rabbit bush and clay hoodoos may be seen. Osprey and eagles frequent the river, sometimes nesting nearby. In winter geese and swans winter along the banks.

Upstream 20 km from Kamloops there is an archeological site consisting of some keekwillie holes, the semi-subterranean dwellings of the Salish Indians. There is no particular season to canoe this river but the months from May to November are the most popular. About half way to Kamloops, Banana Island is passed, easily recognized by its shape. As this is a recreational reserve it is a good place to camp or stop for lunch.

ROUTE - KAMLOOPS LAKE
GRADE - *Lake*
LENGTH - *43 km*
WIDTH - *Approximately 2 km*
VERTICAL DROP - *Nil*
TIME TO ALLOW - *1 day*
NEAREST EMERGENCY COMMUNICATION - *Kamloops or Savona*
CAMPING - ACCOMMODATION - *Unorganized. Provincial government picnic site at Savona*
MAPS - *N.T.S. 1:126,720 92I/NE Kamloops Lake*
HAZARDS - *Wind and some power boats*

DIRECTIONS

Put-in at Riverside Park in Kamloops and take-out at Savona Provincial Park or Highway 1 bridge. Launching and egress points may be reversed.

DESCRIPTION

The first, or eastern portion of this trip is actually on the Thompson river, but it is the only practical access point. Near the river mouth Tranquille is passed on the right bank. One of the first settlers here was William Fortune, an Overlander, who in 1868 had flour mill and later lumber mill here. Later the area was the site of the Provincial Tuberculosis Sanitorium. Further along the north shore is Battle Bluff, Red Point and Painted Bluffs. Near here is a good place to watch for California Bighorn sheep. A herd was started here a few years ago with sheep transplanted from the Chilcotin area.

Savona, on the south side of the lake was originally Savona's Ferry, so named because Francisco Savona had a ferry there. The town is now a lumber town. Take-out at the Provincial Park site on the south shore, east of the town, or just upstream from the highway bridge.

ROUTE - THOMPSON RIVER *Recreational River*
GRADE - *2 with rapids to 3 & 4*
LENGTH - *120 km*
WIDTH - *15 to 50 metres*
VERTICAL DROP - *183 metres*
TIME TO ALLOW - *3 to 5 days*
NEAREST EMERGENCY COMMUNICATION - *Savona, Ashcroft, Spences Bridge and Lytton. Some highway access points along route for emergencies*
CAMPING - ACCOMMODATION - *Unorganized*
MAPS - *N.T.S. 1:126,720 92I/NE Kamloops Lake; 92I/NW Ashcroft; 92I/SW Lytton*
HAZARDS - *Grade 4 rapids, with heavy turbulence and rocks*

DIRECTIONS

Launch at Savona Provincial Park just east of townsite. Take-out on right bank of Fraser just upstream of confluence with Thompson. There is road access to this point.

DESCRIPTION

Only expert paddlers or inflatables should attempt the complete Thompson River trip. All others should plan on pulling out at Ashcroft, Spences Bridge, Goldpan Campsite or Nicomen River. Below this point are grade 4 rapids. It is suggested that only parties of three or more canoes run the river at any point.

This river trip is one of the finest recreational paddles in the province. It passes through country seen from the Trans-Canada Highway, but allows a much closer look and a chance to become part of the river and canyons for a time. The country is part of the Dry Interior Zone, where cactus is common and rattle snakes common enough to watch out for. Some poison ivy grows along the banks so be familiar enough with it to recognize it, and in the spring watch for ticks. Rain is infrequent but the canyons can be chilly on a cloudy day so come prepared with warm clothing and wind proof jackets even though the area is dry.

From Savona to Ashcroft is 38 km. In this section there are approximately seven sets of rapids, depending on water level and how you define rapids. Watch all bridges as they often present problems when pilings have to be dodged. Remember, if in doubt, check it out. Scout ahead. At a rapid just below Kamloops Lake one of the Overlander parties swamped and one man was drowned, just a few days before he would have reached his Cariboo goal. Take all the railroad bridges on the left and highway bridges run through centre.

This section of river passes many historic areas, ranches and towns. Walhachin, once a well irrigated, comfortable prosperous settlement was one of these. Now there are only ghosts. Below there Rattlesnake Hill rises on the right, and at Ashcroft Elephant Hill lies to the north, festooned with radio towers. The Bonaparte river flows in here from the north, and its mouth marks the site of one of the first flour mills in the province. Ashcroft began in 1883 whan a hotel was built in expectation of the railway.

Ashcroft is one place where the trip may be terminated. The next logical take-out point is Spences Bridge, 35 km downstream. Again, be careful of all bridges. About 8 km downstream from Ashcroft is Black Canyon. In some water levels this presents no problem at all except for a few eddies and boils. At other times it forms a large whirlpool that has sucked more than one person under, and then spit them out downstream. It can reach grade 4 water. Watch the sky and river banks here for osprey and eagles that are often seen.

Small rapids occur over the next few kilometres but most are easily skirted on one side or the other. Martel Rapids, 20 km below Black Canyon require scouting as they can be grade 3. Below here are several more small rapids and then Spences bridge. This section is more difficult than the Savona to Ashcroft segment.

There are two good camp spots near Spences bridge. One is on the left bank just below the mouth of the Nicola River. It has good road access. A second is at a waterfall on the right side, downstream of the highway bridge. Road access is not as good here but it is a particularly nice camp spot.

Ten km downstream of Spences bridge there is a government campground on the left bank of the river, Goldpan Park. Canoeists could take-out here. Between Spences bridge there are two grade 3 rapids that must be scouted. Ten km below the campground the Nicoamen River flows in from the left, at the point where the Thompson makes a hard turn to the west. All open canoes should take-out here. The next section is usually run only by kayakers and rafters.

Below this point there is 3 km of grade 4 rapids with the names of: "The Frog", a large rock just below the confluenece; "The Devil's Cutting Board", a rocky section just above the suspension bridge; the "Devil's Cauldron", 100 metres below the suspension bridge and then the "Jaws of Death", an awesome sounding name for the set of rapids where the white water sequences for the British movie "The Trap" was filmed. Oliver Reed was replaced by a local canoeist. Reed merely had water thrown at him in an England based studio.

There are 12 more rough water sections below this rated as grade 3 in low water. They could be run by experts in open boats at low water, but the "Jaws of Death" would have to be portaged. This section of the Thompson now runs through what is called the Pitquah gorge. The highway is no longer near the river but far above. The canyon portion just above Lytton may be viewed from a picnic site across the highway from Skihist Provincial Park and campground.

Elk were transplanted in this area from Jasper a few years ago and have been known to cross the river on occasion, so keep an eye out for them. Watch for bridge pilings which mark the exit from the gorge to the Fraser River. Keep to the right side and take out where the Fraser and Thompson meet, on the right bank of the Thompson. There is road access to this point.

The Indians called this place Camchin, the great fork, the place where the clean blue waters of the Thompson slowly mix with the muddy silt-laden water of the Fraser. When Simon Fraser stopped here on his way to the Pacific he visited a village of over 1200 people. He recorded in his journal of June 20, 1808: "These forks the natives call Camchin, and are formed by a large river which is spoken of so often by our friend the old chief. From an an idea that our friends of the Fort des Prairies department are established upon the sources of it, among the mountains, we gave it the name of Thompson's River."

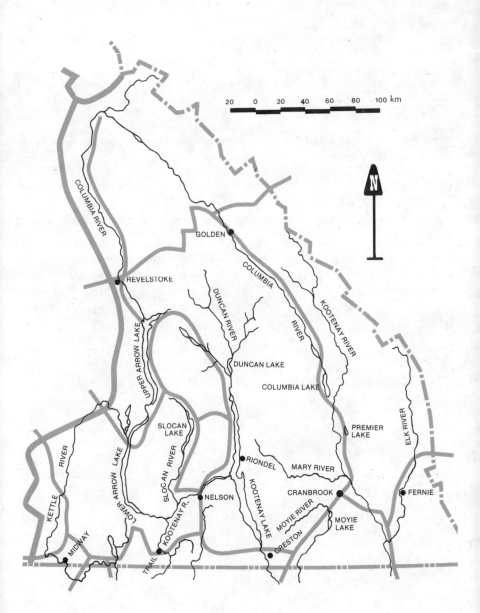

KOOTENAY REGION

ROUTE - KETTLE RIVER - RHONE TO MIDWAY *Natural River*
GRADE - *1 with some rapids to 2*
LENGTH - *50 km*
WIDTH - *20 to 70 metres*
VERTICAL DROP - *Approximately 30 metres*
TIME TO ALLOW - *1 day*
NEAREST EMERGENCY COMMUNICATION - *Rock Creek and Midway*
CAMPING - ACCOMMODATION - *Kettle River Recreation Area, just north of Rock Creek on Highway 33. 48 campsites. Rock Creek Park also has a few campsites and pit toilets.*
MAPS - *N.T.S 1:125,00 82E/SW; Penticton 82E/SE Grand Forks*
HAZARDS - *Wood spillway at Boundary Sawmills, small rapids*

DIRECTIONS

Travel east on Highway 3 from Osoyoos to Rock Creek. Turn north on Highway 33 for 26 km where a road to the right leads to the former settlement of Rhone. 1.25 km along this road a bridge crosses the West Kettle. This will be the highest point at which launching will be feasible. It is also possible to launch at Westbridge and the old Zamora Mill Site, both of which are south of the Rhone put-in. Take-out at Midway where a bridge crosses the Kettle.

DESCRIPTION

The Kettle is a pleasant river trip, passing through pastoral land with cattle and mixed farming. There are lots of short rapids which in medium to low water are relatively safe for the novice paddler. High water could change these to grade 3, perhaps even 4.

The settlement of Rhone, now really just a collection of old buildings was a station on the old Kettle Valley line which used this route to reach the Okanagan Valley and Hope. Completed in 1916 much of the line has since been abandoned.

At Rock Creek there are old mine tunnels and placer workings that can be explored, reminders of the big rush to this small creek in 1860. It was this rush which prompted the building of the Dewdney Trail. Rock Creek can be recognized by a trestle bridge crossing the Kettle and the collection of buildings around the highway junction. 4.2 km downstream of Rock Creek is the Ingram Creek bridge, an alternate pull-out point. 10 km below this watch for a sign reading: "Caution, Boaters. Drop Structure Ahead." On the right bank is a sign: "Portage", and then "Portage Here", marking a 30 metre carry. The drop is caused by a wooden spillway built for the Boundary Sawmill.

The Kettle River was called the Colvile River by early fur traders, and the "Ne-hoi-al-pit-qua" by the native Indians. *1001 B.C. Place Names* gives two theories of the name Kettle; one that it comes from the Kettle Falls, known as "La Chaudiere" to early explorere, and second that it comes from the round holes, shaped like kettles, which have been hollowed out in the rocks by water erosion.

The paddle from Rhone to Midway passes through an area that offers one of the most spectacular displays of autumn leaves in the province. Lined with cottonwoods, aspen and birches the river viewpoint heightens the fall grandeur.

Midway, the take-out point, was laid out as a townsite in 1893, and given the name Boundary City. Being similar to the nearby town of Boundary Falls it was changed to Midway, a suitable name as it was midway between Penticton and Marcus, Washington, its nearest railway point; midway from Hope to Wild Horse Creek on the Dewdney Trail; and midway between the Rockies and the Pacific. For canoes it is not midway, it is the terminus. The easiest take-out is at the bridge in the centre of town. There is accommodation and supplies at Greenwood, 13 km east.

ROUTE - CRESTON VALLEY
GRADE - *1 and lake*
LENGTH - *45 km*
WIDTH - *50 metres to 1 km*
VERTICAL DROP - *Minimal*
TIME TO ALLOW - *1 to 3 days*
NEAREST EMERGENCY COMMUNICATION - *Creston*
CAMPING - ACCOMMODATION - *Unorganized*
MAPS - *N.T.S. 1:126,720 82F/SE Creston*
HAZARDS - *None*

DIRECTIONS

Access from Canada-U.S.A. border on Highway 21. Put-in here and canoe downriver, north, toward Kootenay Lake. Take-out on east side of Kootenay Lake along Highway 3.

DESCRIPTION

This route follows a meandering section of the Kootenay River which connects several interesting sloughs and waterways. The valley area is one of the most picturesque in Southeastern B.C. and is the resting and nesting place for thousands of waterfowl.

The southern part of the river passes Indian Reserve and farmland, and is confined by dykes in some areas. Below the highway bridge a few kilometres the river channel splits into two. A left channel may be taken into Leach Lake and the right to Duck Lake. Six Mile Slough at the end of Kootenay Lake is also worth exploring.

This area is known as Creston Flats and a stop-of-interest sign gives a brief history of the area.

"It was the dream, in the 1880's of W.A. Baillie-Grohman, British sportsman and financier, to reclaim these fertile flats from the annual river floods. His canal at Canal Flats (in the east Kootenays) diverted part of the Kootenay into the Columbia but was abandoned. The first succesful reclamation was in 1893. Now 25,110 acres lie secure beyond 53 miles of dykes."

More recently the valley has become an area managed closely for migratory waterfowl by the federal and provincial governments. Spring and fall paddlers will see thousands upon thousands of birds here including most species of ducks, geese and swans. Be careful not to disturb feeding flocks or nesting birds while canoeing.

ROUTE - SLOCAN RIVER
GRADE - *2 with some grade 3*
LENGTH - *60 km*
WIDTH - *n/a*
VERTICAL DROP - *n/a*
TIME TO ALLOW - *1 day*
NEAREST EMERGENCY COMMUNICATION - *Slocan and small communities along the route; Highway 6 follows the river*
CAMPING - ACCOMMODATION - *Camping unorganized along route. Accommodation at Slocan, Winlaw and Cresent Valley*
MAPS - *N.T.S 1:250,000 82F Nelson*
HAZARDS - *Sweepers, log jams and some fast water*

DIRECTIONS

From Highway 3 between Castlegar and Nelson, turn up Highway 6 to Slocan. Launch here and take out at the highway crossing where the Slocan River flows into the Kootenay.

DESCRIPTION

Limited information was available for this route. It is reported to present few problems for experienced canoeists and to be ideal for kayaks and rubber inflatables. Canoeists must be ready to scout all doubtful areas and proceed cautiously.

The name Slocan is reported to come from the Shuswap Indian word "slok-ken", meaning frogs, or "slokam", meaning to catch salmon.

ROUTE - MOYIE LAKE
GRADE - *Lake*
LENGTH - *13 km*
WIDTH - *1 km*

VERTICAL DROP - *Nil*
TIME TO ALLOW - *One day*
NEAREST EMERGENCY COMMUNICATION - *Moyie, on southern lake*
CAMPING - ACCOMMOCATION - *Camping at Moyie Lake Provincial Park, launching site. Accommodation at Moyie or Cranbrook*
MAPS - *N.T.S 1:126,720 82G/SW Elko*
HAZARDS - *Heavy winds at times and power boats*

DIRECTIONS

Put-in at Moyie Lake Provincial Park, 20 km south of Cranbrook on Highway 3/95. Take-out at same point or at Highway bridge crossing the Moyie River just south of the lake outfall.

DESCRIPTION

Moyie Lake is actually two lakes, joined by a two kilometer stretch of the Moyie River. Each section is approximately 6 km in length. This is a popular area for water skiiers and power boaters so in that respect is not a prime canoeing area. Fishing is good for kokanee, rainbow trout and Dolly Varden.

The Moyie system has gone through a number of name changes, starting with McDonald's River, a name given it by David Thompson after his clerk Finan McDonald. Governor Simpson called it the "Grand Quete" to honor the chief of an Indian tribe. The present name comes from the French "Mouille", meaning wet, a term applied to the valley.

On the west side of the lake is the abandoned St. Eugene Mine, just west of Moyie. The mine was discovered by a Kootenay Indian, and developed by Father Coccola who with the proceeds of mineral claims built a new mission church. The development of the lead-silver mine influenced the expansion of Cominco and the construction of the Crowsnest Pass Railway according to a roadside stop of interest sign.

ROUTE - MOYIE RIVER
GRADE - *1 to 3*
LENGTH - *50 km*
WIDTH - *15 metres*
VERTICAL DROP - *Approximately 110 metres*
TIME TO ALLOW - *6 hours, 1 day*
NEAREST EMERGENCY COMMUNICATION - *Moyie, Yahk and Kingsgate border crossing*
CAMPING - ACCOMMODATION - *Moyie Lake Provincial Park at head of lake, and Yahk Provincial Park at Yahk. Unorganized along rest of the route*
MAPS - *N.T.S. 1:126,720 82G/SW Elko; 82F/SE Creston*
HAZARDS - *Grade 3 rapids, sweepers, log jams*

DIRECTIONS

Put-in anywhere on Moyie Lake and paddle south to river outlet. There are numerous access points along the river though the trip is usually terminated at Yahk or Kingsgate.

DESCRIPTION

The paddle down the Moyie River is scenic, popular and exciting, with the possibility of swamping in highwater and scraping bottom in low water. The section from the lake to Yahk is relatively slow with a section of rapids at the 15 km point. Below Yahk the speed of the River increases enough that this section is used for a raft race during the Yahk May Day celebrations.

Wildlife includes whitetail and mule deer, coyote, black bear as well as birds such as mergansers, mallards, Canada geese and numerous small song birds in the shoreline fields and bush. Fishing is fair.

The name Yahk does not come from an Asian beast of burden but from a Kootenay Indian word, "yaak", meaning bow. This name was used for the Kootenay river which formed a bow shape and the name came to mean the country within the bow of the river.

ROUTE - ST MARY'S RIVER

GRADE - *2 with grade 3 to 4 rapids in highwater*
LENGTH - *56 km*
WIDTH - *100 metres*
VERTICAL DROP - *215 metres*
TIME TO ALLOW - *1 to 2 days*
NEAREST EMERGENCY COMMUNICATION - *Marysville, Wycliffe or Fort Steele at the terminus.*
CAMPING - ACCOMMODATION - *Unorganized*
MAPS - *N.T.S. 1:126,720 82G/NW Cranbrook; 82F/NE Kaslo*
HAZARDS - *Rapids of grade 3 to 4 in high water*

DIRECTIONS

From Cranbrook take Highway 95 toward Marysville and Kimberly. At Marysville continue west up the St. Mary's River to St. Mary's Lake. Put-in at the lake and paddle downriver to Fort Steele on the Kootenay.

DESCRIPTION

Limited information was available on this canoe route except that in high water there is some grade 3 and 4 water. Paddlers must be sure to check out the river as they go.

The trip starts at St. Mary's Lake, 3 km by 0.5 km, about 20 km west of Marysville. The river was named for the Blessed Virgin Mary, patron saint of the Oblates of Mary Immaculate. It was named by Father Fouquet, OMI, who founded the St. Eugene Mission in 1874. The mission is passed approximately half way between Wycliffe and Fort Steele. The mission was named after a name-saint of the founder of the order, Charles Joseph Eugene de Mazenod.

The river and lake are good fishing by fly or spinning lure for cutthroat, Dollies and rainbow trout to 450 grams.

At the Kootenay river a take-out can be arranged at the highway bridge, or canoeists could land below Fort Steele.

ROUTE - ELK RIVER
GRADE - 2
LENGTH - *Approximately 200 km*
WIDTH - *Averages 50 metres*
VERTICAL DROP - *Approximately 600 metres*
TIME TO ALLOW - *5 days*
NEAREST EMERGENCY COMMUNICATION - *Sparwood, Fernie, Elko and Highway 3 between Sparwood and Elko*
CAMPING ACCOMMODATION - *Camping unorganized along route. Accommodation at Natal and Fernie*
MAPS - *N.T.S. 1:126,720 82J/SW-SE Canal Flats; 82G/NW-NE Cranbrook; 82G/SW Elko*
HAZARDS - *Log jams and sweepers*

DIRECTIONS

From Natal on Highway 3 take the secondary road north toward Elkford. Continue north to the headwaters of the river and a suitable launching point. Take-out at any point along the route or at Elko on Highway 3.

DESCRIPTION

Only limited information was available on this river so canoeists should proceed with some caution. The entire course of the river is reported canoeable but highwater changes it from year to year. Watch for log jams and sweepers and scout ahead if there is any doubt.

The river was named the "Stag River" by David Thompson for the large number of elk or wapiti that could be seen along the valley. Although it is still a good wildlife area prime regions are being lost to strip mining for coal. Mines are clearly evident in much of the region. Other wildlife in the region includes whitetail deer, black bear and bighorn sheep, as well as the more usual smaller mammals.

Before the flooding of the Kootenay **River behind the Libby dam, a** take-out point would have been on the Kootenay. Now it is best to pull-out at Elko on Highway 3.

ROUTE - PREMIER LAKE
GRADE - *Lake*
LENGTH - *4 km*
WIDTH - *1 km*
VERTICAL DROP - *Nil. Elevation 870 metres*
TIME TO ALLOW - *½ to 1 day*
NEAREST EMERGENCY COMMUNICATION - *Skookumchuck 13 km west*
CAMPING - ACCOMMODATION - *Premier Lake Provincial Park at south end of lake, 41 campsites*
MAPS - *N.T.S. 1:126,720 82G/NW Cranbrook*
HAZARDS - *None*

DIRECTIONS

Go north 0.8 km from Skookumchuck on Highway 93-95 then turn east 16 km on a narrow gravel road. Put-in at Provincial park.

DESCRIPTION

Premier Lake lies at the western foot of the Rocky Mountains. Scenery is spectacular and wildlife is frequently seen. There is good fishing for rainbow trout and Eastern brook trout.

Quartz Lake lies approximately 3 km south on the same road. It is popular with local fishermen angling for rainbow trout. The lake is small for canoeing, 1.5 km by 0.4 km, but could offer an interesting paddle for anyone camped at Premier Lake.

ROUTE - KOOTENAY RIVER - GIBRALTAR TO FORT STEELE
GRADE - *2, rapids to 3*
LENGTH - *96 km*
WIDTH - *15 to 100 metres*
VERTICAL DROP - *49 metres*
TIME TO ALLOW - *2 to 3 days*
NEAREST EMERGENCY COMMUNICATION - *Canal Flats, Skookumchuck, Wasa bridge, Fort Steele*
CAMPING - ACCOMMODATION - *Thunder Hill Provincial Park at Canal Flats, and Wasa Lake Provincial Park. Unorganized camping along route.*
MAPS - *N.T.S. 1:126,720 82G/NW Cranbrook; 82 J/SW Canal Flats*
HAZARDS - *Sweepers, deadheads and rapids*

DIRECTIONS

From Canal Flats on Highway 93-95 proceed up the Kootenay River on a secondary road to the area of Gibraltar Rock, 27 km. Put-in here and take out at Fort Steele.

DESCRIPTION

The Kootenay River trip is one which passes through a region of wilderness character, with scenery unsurpassed anywhere in the province. Wildlife is abundant and hazards are few.

Above the put-in point the river has grade 4 to 5 water so it is not recommended for the casual paddler, or in fact any open boat. Below Gibraltar Rock though, the river is relatively easy for experienced paddlers and those who take their time to check out the few rapids that appear. Most of these fast spots are wide and shallow though in a few spots the river flows into rock walls that make for sharp turns and some whirlpools. These are easily seen ahead of time and can be portaged.

As the Kootenay flows south it slows until by the time Wasa is reached the water is slow. At Fort Steele there is one set of rapids that are sometimes grade 3. They can be portaged on the east bank. The St. Mary's River flows in from the west so avoid portaging on that side.

Two raft races are held on the Kootenay. The first is part of the Kimberley Beer Festival and is usually held in July. It runs from Canal Flats to Fort Steele. The second is usually in August and runs from Bummer's Flats to Fort Steele as part of the Sam Steele celebrations at Cranbrook.

Along the route of the Kootenay the place-names add to the history of the country for canoeists. Canal Flats was the site of a canal dug by Baillie-Grohman in an attempt to lower the lake level at Creston. The canal connected the Kootenay river to Columbia Lake over the height of land that separated the two. Earlier David Thompson had referred to it as "McGillivray's portage". Baillie-Grohman's scheme failed when the federal government restricted the plans so much that the canal became unusable.

The name of the Kootenay River itself, spelt in a number of ways, comes from the Indians. "Co" means water, and "tinneh" means people. Early travellers referred to them as the Lake Indians. David Thompson called this McGillivray's River but the name did not stick.

Skookumchuck Creek means literally strong water in the Chinook jargon of the early traders. This could be interpreted as turbulent water or water with a lot of rapids. Ta Ta Creek is supposed to be named after an early robber who waved Ta Ta as he disappeared across the creek. Wasa was named by settler Nils Hanson after Vasa, a coastal town in Finland.

Finally comes Fort Steele, the site of the North West Mounted Police post established by Major Sam Steele in 1887. Formerly called Galbraith's ferry the settlement was renamed to honor the Major. The reconstruction is an interesting place for any traveller to visit.

ROUTE - COLUMBIA RIVER - COLUMBIA LAKE TO DONALD STATION
GRADE - *1*
LENGTH - *235 km*
WIDTH - *n/a*

VERTICAL DROP - *10 metres approximately*
TIME TO ALLOW - *3 to 5 days*
NEAREST EMERGENCY COMMUNICATION - *Athalmere, Golden or Donald Station*
CAMPING - ACCOMMODATION - *Unorganized*
MAPS - *N.T.S. 1:250,000 82J Kananaskis Lakes; 82K Lardeau; 82N Golden*
HAZARDS - *None*

DIRECTIONS

Put-in on Columbia Lake or where Highway 93-95 crosses the river near Fairmont Hot Springs. Take-out is possible at several small settlements or road crossings, or at the route's end at Donald Station highway crossing.

DESCRIPTION

This long section of the Columbia headwaters is one of the few sections of the Columbia that have not been affected by one or more dams. It is a pleasant paddle past marshes, side-channels and sloughs filled with wildlife and birds such as ospreys, eagles, great blue herons, ravens, grouse, ducks, geese and swans. Grass-covered hills border part of the river and high clay bluffs other parts, each offering a certain type of habitat for animals.

Campsites and meal spots are easily found on the gravel and sand bars. Be sure to ask permission to camp if it is private land. In some places along the river there is evidence of the early settlers who came here and stayed, and everywhere there is the feeling of history, of David Thompson and all the fur traders, trappers and voyageurs who first used the broad stream. Along the banks, beaver, moose, elk and deer may be seen as much of the route passes through land sparsely populated and undisturbed enough to still provide suitable habitat.

Anglers will find a few rainbow and Dollies at stream mouths, and even some ling cod and sturgeon.

A good map will be a help on this route as often the river channel all but disappears in a mass of riverside lakes and side channels. The route is a good one for beginner river paddlers or for family trips, yet even the most experienced will enjoy the slow pace of the river and its life.

In the 1880's W.A. Baillie-Grohman had a scheme for a canal from the Kootenay River across to the Columbia system at Canal Flats. His idea was to control Kootenay flooding and provide more agricultural land at Creston. B.C. Hydro are now proposing a similar scheme. Their idea is to use the Kootenay water to increase the storage behind the Mica and newly proposed Revelstoke dams. Such a diversion would wipe out much of the above described river and marshes, one of B.C.'s major resting places for migratory waterfow. The reduced flows would also have an adverse affect on the Kootenay system.

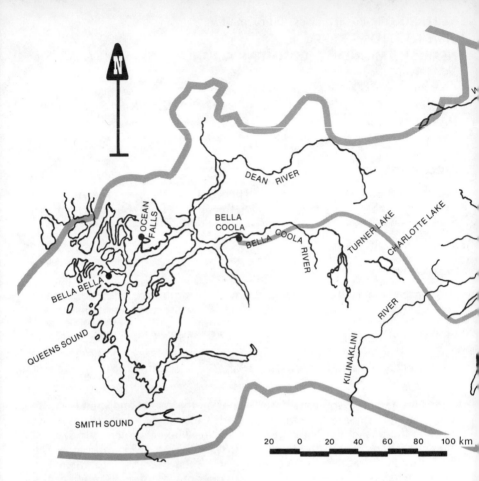

CARIBOO REGION

ROUTE - CHILKO LAKE *Scenic Shoreline*
GRADE - *Lake*
LENGTH - *195 km return*
WIDTH - *0.5 to 5 km*
VERTICAL DROP - *Nil*
TIME TO ALLOW - *1 to 2 weeks*
NEAREST EMERGENCY COMMUNICATION - *Chilko Lake Lodge at north end or Alexis Creek, 95 km north east*
CAMPING - ACCOMMODATION - *B.C.F.S. campsite at north end of lake; Chilko Lodge and unorganized primitive sites along the lake*
MAPS - *N.T.S. 1:250,000 92N Mount Waddington; 92N/9E Tatlayoko Lake; 92N/8E Stikelan Creek; 92N/1E Chilko Mountain*
HAZARDS - *Frequent high winds and cold water*

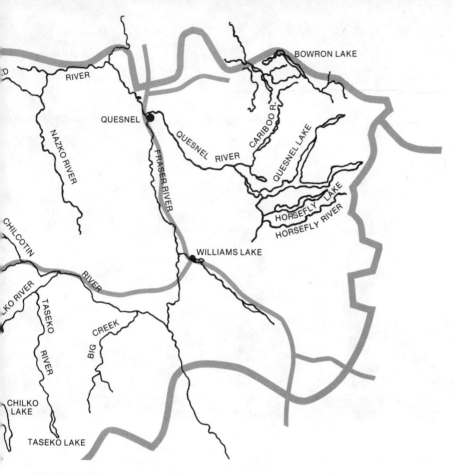

DIRECTIONS

From Williams Lake drive east on the Bella Coola Road to Alexis Creek. The shortest route is to turn south along the Chilko River 15 km west of Alexis Creek over a rough dusty road. From Williams Lake this route is 195 km. The second route is to continue to Tatla Lake and then drive south to the Choelquoit Lake road, which heads east to the Chilko Road. This is 370 km. A third route is to travel the Taseko Lake road from Hanceville to the Nemaia Valley Road. This route heads west to Chilko Lake at Canoe Point, and half way along the east side. This is not as good a place to leave vehicles as Chilko Lake lodge.

DESCRIPTION

Chilko Lake is a remote, wilderness lake, very susceptible to high winds and should only be paddled by experienced canoeists with wilderness camping knowledge. Be prepared to spend days wind bound. High winds make it unlikely that the entire lake could be paddled in a week. The lake is glacier fed and the water extremely cold. July and August are the best months, when the winds are lowest.

The canoe journey is best begun at the north end of the lake, at Chilko Lodge. Be sure to launch in the lake and not the widened river or paddling will be difficult. In the fall Indians will be fishing for salmon near the outlet at centuries old fishing stands.

Along the lake are several good places to stop, such as the Big Lagoon about a third of the way down the west side. Bateman Island, at the entrance to 9 km long Franklyn Arm has a small cabin suitable for an overnight stop. On the east side is Duff Island, the film site of Disney's *The Bears and I,* and just north of here is Canoe Point and the Nemaia Indian Reserve, although the village is a few miles east.

Near the south end glaciers and mountains tower above the shores. Chilko Mountain, 2700 metres high; Good Hope Mountain, 3200 metres; Farrow Glacier and Goddard Glacier can all be seen by paddlers. Wildlife includes, moose, deer and grizzly and fishing is good for rainbow and Dolly Varden.

Chilko Lake has been proposed by B.C. Hydro as a power project. A dam at the north end would virtually eliminate the river while a tunnel through the southern mountains would empty water into Bute Inlet to generate power. Fortunately this would affect salmon runs to such an extent that it may never be constructed.

ROUTE - CHILKO RIVER *Natural River*

GRADE - *1 to 5*

LENGTH - *84 km*

WIDTH - *5 to 30 metres*

VERTICAL DROP - *450 metres*

TIME TO ALLOW - *2 to 3 days*

NEAREST EMERGENCY COMMUNICATION - *Alexis Creek, 96 km from lake, and Chilko Lake lodge*

CAMPING - ACCOMMODATION - *B.C.F.S. campsite at outlet of lake. Unorganized elsewhere. None in Lava Canyon*

MAPS - *N.T.S. 1:50,000 92N/9E Tatlayoko Lake; 92N/16E Eagle Lake; 920/13W&E Scum Lake; 93B/4E Redstone; 93B/3W Alexis Creek*

HAZARDS - *Grade 5 rapids, cold water*

DIRECTIONS

Follow directions to Chilko Lake. Launch at outfall of lake. Take-out above Lava Canyon, unless an expert paddler in closed boat. Take-out at Chilko-Taseko junction or Alexis Creek if expert.

DESCRIPTION

The Chilko River is one of the most attractive and varied rivers in the province, and when combined with a trip down the Chilcotin is the finest river trip in Canada. Its many attributes made it one of first to be suggested as a suitable candidate for "Wild River" legislation back in 1967. The salmon run alone serves to make it rather unique for while most salmon rivers have a run every four years the Chilko has two major runs in four years and two minor runs. The major runs see 500,000 sockeye spawning in the gravel where the current quickens at the lake's exit. This amounts to one third of the Fraser River's total. In fact the salmon have helped preserve the river and lake, so far, from hydro electric development. One proposed scheme would divert Taseko Lake water into Chilko Lake, dam Chilko Lake at the exit and drill a tunnel through the south mountains to the Southgate river. What has eluded engineers and ichthyologists so far is how to transport millions of fry from their spawning beds, into the lake for the first year of life, and then back into a dried up river for their journey down to the sea.

Historically the river has been used for fishing by the natives, and even in some of the seemingly inaccessible places in the Canyon there are trails to fishing sites. It is extremely unlikely that the river was used for transportation. Generally it was considered unrunnable until 1970 when a 12 foot inflatable made what is thought to be the first passage through Lava Canyon, and then not without extreme difficulty. Now the river is frequently run by commercial rafting companies. Sections are suitable for paddling in open boats.

The trip starts in Chilko Lake, 1173 metres above sea level and drops to 732 metres at the confluence with the Chilcotin. For paddlers it is best described in three sections; Chilko Lake to Lava Canyon; Lava Canyon; and Taseko junction to Chilcotin junction.

For 40 km from the outfall of the lake to Lava Canyon the Chilko offers pleasant canoeing. The drop is 138 metres with grade 1 to 2 water. Hazards include the cold glacial water, sweepers, some boulders in mid stream and a bridge. Henry's Crossing, once called Henry's Ford, is a bridge to the east side of the river, and is about half way to the take-out. Take-out is just beyond a farm on the left bank; a spot where the road reaches riverside. This should be checked out ahead of time by vehicle. Ahead will be the first canyon walls, about 15 metres high. Pull out on the left bank. If this take-out is missed you will be in Lava Canyon and there is no way to carry out. On this first section of river you are likely to see deer, moose, bald eagles, spawning salmon and Indian fishermen, mergansers, shorebirds and many others. Wildlife is best seen early in the morning.

Lava Canyon must not be attempted by open canoes. Closed boats and inflatables should only attempt the canyon if paddlers are experienced and strong. The velocity approaches 24 km per hour, egress is difficult to impossible, resting spots are almost non-existant and there are many continuous grade 5 rapids. There will be no chance to scout rapids and no place to rest for the next 24 km. In 24 km the river drops 215 metres, 9 metres per km. The canyon was formed as the river eroded its way through centuries old lava flows that covered much of this area. The banks are now 60 metres high, sometimes vertical rock walls, sometimes eroded with loose skree at the angle of repose.

The first rapid in the canyon is just below the suggested take-out point for open canoes. From up river it appears like a water-fall, with a sharp left S bend. On both sides of the river are boulders and broken rock with huge souse holes. Stay in the middle. In fact, stay in the middle of the river for the whole canyon. This first rapid is the steepest drop, but there are four more distinct drops interspersed with grade 3 and 4 water. The canyon has continuous heavy water with haystacks in the middle and rocks and holes on both sides. Sometimes small water falls appear on the side of the channel. About 2 km above the Taseko junction the river levels out. Just upstream of the junction a cable car crosses the Chilko. Allow at least half a day for the canyon.

The third section of the Chilko will seem anticlimactic after the excitement of the canyon. This section can be paddled by open canoes with caution, but be careful to watch for Siwash Bridge and "The Gut". Access to the junction is from the Chilko River road. From the Highway 20 turn-off follow up the river for 16 km. Watch for a left turn and then drive a further 6.5 km, dropping down to the river at the junction.

From the junction the river is easy for the first 6.5 km, though standing waves may have to be avoided by paddling close to shore. With the inflow of the Taseko water, volumes have doubled to between 28 and 280 cubic metres per second. River velocity is between 6 and 11 km per hour. The river drops 90 metres in this 20 km stretch. Beyond the 6.5 kilometer point there are two S bends which could offer some difficulty, but they can usually be run on the right. Below this, at kilometre 13 is Siwash bridge and "The Gut", a small canyon about 5 metres wide which must be portaged. An easy portage is on the right. This canyon is usually grade 4, but at other times forms a virtual waterfall as water backs up and then surges through.

Below the Gut 0.5 km the river slows and is flanked by wide, open fields. On the left is the site of old Fort Chilcotin, an outpost of Fort Alexandria. Nothing remains of the fort now. Soon the Chilcotin river flows in from the west, almost unnoticed, adding its insignificant flow to the huge volume of the Chilko.

Egress is possible anywhere along Highway 20, or at the Alexis Creek bridge. Paddlers continuing downstream should see the description under the Chilcotin River, mainstream.

ROUTE - TASEKO RIVER *Natural River*
GRADE - *2 to 6*
LENGTH - *100 km*
WIDTH - *20 to 50 metres*
VERTICAL DROP - *550 metres*
TIME TO ALLOW - *1 to 3 days*
NEAREST EMERGENCY COMMUNICATION - *Alexis Creek 150 km from Taseko; by road 100 km to Hanceville or Lees Corner*
CAMPING - ACCOMMODATION - *Unorganized*
MAPS - *N.T.S 1:250,000 920 Taseko Lakes*
HAZARDS - *Grade 6 rapids with difficult portages, remote, cold water*

DIRECTIONS

Take Bella Coola Road west from Williams Lake to Lee's Corner and then the Engineer's Road south west 100 km to Taseko Lake. Take-out at Taseko-Chilko junction or Alexis Creek.

DESCRIPTION

The locals name for this river is "The Whitewater", in fact Taseko means whitewater in the Indian dialect of the Chilcotin. That in itself should be an indication of what the river is like. Yet canoeists have started out on the river with no advance knowledge and wrecked in the rough downstream water. It is not a river to be attempted by the inexperienced. It has been succesfully run by kayakers and could be by expert paddlers in open Canadians willing to portage many rapids.

From the put-in at Taseko Lake to the bridge crossing the Taseko is Grade 2 to 3, with definite grade 3 in a canyon about 4 km above the bridge to Konni Lakes and Nemaia Valley. This 32 km section can be terminated at the bridge, and should be unless you are an expert paddler. Below here is continuous grade 2 with grade 4 to 5 rapids opposite Scum Lake and 3 grade 6 rapids within the last 30 km, approaching the confluence of the Taseko and Chilko Rivers. These rapids can be portaged. It is imperative that every bend and rapid be scouted before running.

The Taseko water is glacier fed and therefore cold and silty. River velocity is 3 to 12 kilometres per hour, with a volume of 14 - 170 cubic metres per second.

Like the Chilco River the Taseko passes through an area once covered by lava from volcanoes, although there is no lava canyon such as on the former river. Wildlife likely to be seen includes, black bear, deer, moose, bald eagles, beaver, mergansers and various shorebirds.

There is road access to the junction of the Taseko and Chilko, on the west side of the Chilko, and a good campsite. Other access is south on the Chilko or at Alexis Creek. See the Chilko description if you are to continue down river as there is one impassable section.

ROUTE - CHILCOTIN RIVER - UPPER SECTION *Natural River*
GRADE - *1 to 4*
LENGTH - *72 km*
WIDTH - *10 to 50 metres*
VERTICAL DROP - *335 metres; Average 4.6 metres per km*
TIME TO ALLOW - *2 to 3 days*
NEAREST EMERGENCY COMMUNICATION - *Redstone and Alexis Creek*
CAMPING - ACCOMMODATION - *Unorganized. Much private land so ask permission*
MAPS - *N.T.S. 1:50,000 93B/4E&W Redstone; 93B/3W Alexis Creek*
HAZARDS - *Rapids, windfalls, log jams*

DIRECTIONS

Take Highway 20 west from Williams Lake to Alexis Creek. About 28 km past Alexis Creek a road goes north to Chilcotin Lake. The road is just west of a bridge over the Chilcotin River. The lake is 48 km northwest.

DESCRIPTION

The upper section of the Chilcotin, before its confluence with the Chilko is so unlike the rest of the river that it is necessary to describe it on its own. The volume of water for instance, is only 1/10th that of the main stream. The 72 km of river is difficult and tiresome to paddle, not because of danger but rather the number of small obstacles that occur and the low volume of water.

The route starts in Chilcotin Lake on the Fraser Plateau at an elevation of 1070 metres and drops to 732 at the Chilko. It flows across the Fraser Plateau, through an area of lava flow and volcanic rock. On this upper section there tends to be much more riverside growth such as willow and poplar, unlike the semi-arid conditions found downstream. There are spruce and lodgepole pine, some sage, and a wide variety of grasses. Wildlife likely to be seen includes moose, mule deer, and black bear. The area is an excellent one for fishing, with rainbow trout to two kg being caught in Chilcotin Lake.

Paddlers should launch in the lake and paddle east to the exit and beginning of the river. The first 6.5 km has fast water with shallow rapids, followed by 8 km of slow water through rangeland. Then another 1.5 km of fast water followed by 10 km of easy canoeing. At this point a 10 metre wide canyon, 4.5 km long is entered with a drop of 10 metres per mile. A series of boulder fields and ledges make it difficult to canoe, but lining is possible. There are also two windfalls here that block the river. A boulder field south of the canyon preceeds a 4 km run past the settlement of Redstone, below which the Chilanko River enters from the west. Here the river separates into a number of narrow and shallow channels for a distance of 15 km. These are often blocked by windfalls. A log jam 5 km above the Chilko Lake road bridge can usually be bypassed to the right. Some lining may be necessary here. The last 7 km to the confluence consists of narrow channels, rock gardens and log jams, with a drop of 7.5 metres per km.

Egress is simple near the confluence as Highway 20 follows most of the Chilcotin River. Flowing in from the right is the Chilko River, wide, cold and strong with ten times the volume of the warm Chilcotin. The name Chilcotin means people of the Chilco, which has been translated as meaning either "warm water" of "young man's river". The warm water must obviously refer to the Chilcotin's upper section rather than the frigid Chilko. A description of the lower, main-stream continues.

ROUTE - CHILCOTIN RIVER - MAIN-STREAM *Natural River*

GRADE - *1 to 5*

LENGTH - *106 km to junction with Fraser; additional 27 km to take-out*

WIDTH - *30 metres, narrowing to 10 in canyons*

VERTICAL DROP - *366 metres to confluence with Fraser*

TIME TO ALLOW - *3 to 4 days*

NEAREST EMERGENCY COMMUNICATION - *Alexis Creek and Riske Creek; downstream nearest point is Gang Ranch Road*

CAMPING - ACCOMMODATION - *Unorganized*

MAPS - *N.T.S. 1:50,000 93B/3E&W Alexis Creek; 920/15E Hanceville; 920/15E&W Riske Creek; 920/16W Springhouse; 920/9W Dog Creek*

HAZARDS - *Grade 5 + rapids*

DIRECTIONS

From Williams Lake head west on Highway 20, the Bella Coola Road, to 16 km west of Alexis Creek. Access to the River is anywhere along the road. Take-out can be Hanceville or Farwell Canyon. Only expert paddlers in closed boats or inflatables should venture into the Chilcotin Canyon as the Grade 5 + rapids are practically impossible to line or portage.

DESCRIPTION

This section of river, combined with either the Taseko, Chilko or upper Chilcotin is one of the most interesting, exciting and pleasant river trips in British Columbia. Interesting because of the varied land forms, flora and fauna that is encountered, exciting because of the grade 3 to 5 rapids, and pleasant because of the semi-arid region's lack of rain, mosquitoes and other noxious pests. Historically the river was the home of the warring Chilcotins. Later it became the main access to the Chilcotin country for miners and then ranchers, the mainstay of the rolling grassland. Though not a wilderness river few people will be seen, save perhaps a few whitewater rafters.

The paddle begins upstream of Alexis Creek and although it is described in a continuous manner there are three major sections: launch point to Hanceville; Hanceville to Farwell Canyon; and Farwell to the Fraser and Gang Ranch take-out. The volume is now ranging from a low of 340 cu.m/sec. to 3400 cu.m/sec., increasing all the way to the Fraser. The river is about 7 metres deep with an average flow of 8 km/h.

Kilometre zero is the junction of the Chilko and Chilcotin. From here to Hanceville Bridge at 46 km is generally an easy paddle. At 5.6 km Bull Canyon and Battle Mountain are passed without any river problems. At 12.5 km there is an S curve with grade 3 rapids in some water levels. The standing waves in midstream can usually be easily avoided. 3.5 km downstream is the Alexis Creek bridge to Highway 20. Then the river broadens and winds past Anahim Flats, site of the Anahim Indian Reserve. At Stoney Canyon, 35 km, there is some fast water in a chute and then easy canoeing again the the Hanceville Bridge at 45 km. Take-out below the bridge on the left bank.

Hanceville is a group of ranch buildings on a flat above and to the north of the river. A couple of kilometres north on the bridge road is Lee's Corner, a store and restaurant. To the south is Chilko Ranch.

The next section of river, to Farwell Canyon, has lots of grade 3 water and is suitable only for experienced paddlers. This stretch is 46 km in length with an average drop of 3.3 metres per kilometre.

Just below the bridge, at 45 km, there is a set of rapids called Old Bridge Rapids, named after the remains of the old Hanceville bridge that was washed out in an ice jam and now sits on shore. At 48 km the Goosenecks are entered and Hanceville Canyon. Where there is a large bluff to the left pull over and explore a bat cave that is on the left bank. A small eddy just down river provides a pull-out. The Gooseneck rapids continue for a few kilometres and then the river levels out to grade 1 and 2 until 77 km and Big Creek. Stop upstream of the confluence and check out the grade 3 rapids just downstream. Big Creek can be waded upstream. The long rapid ahead drops 15 metres in 0.5 kilometres. On the downstream side of Big Creek, on the right bank, lies the abandoned Brown homestead. Across the river is the Wineglass Ranch.

For an excellent view of the river stop here and climb the open grass hill to the south, 305 metres above the river. Downstream, at 88 km, watch for a fence on the right and a bend left with large cottonwoods screening farm fields. This is the pull-out for Farwell Canyon, easily reached by road. This spot is the take-out for all but the most experienced paddlers in closed boats and some inflatables. The road crosses the river and provides access to Riske Creek and Highway 20 to the north.

Farwell canyon is a good spot to camp and explore for a day or two. An old homestead, sculpted sandhill hoodoos, a massive sanddune on the north side, Indian pictographs on a rock above the road, and wildlife such as bighorn sheep, weasels, black bear, mule deer, coyotes, longbilled curlews, eagles, ducks, geese and many others all combine to make the canyon a unique spot on the river.

The 18 kilometre river trip from Farwell to the Fraser is relatively short and fast. Farwell is grade 4 to 5 with a speed of about 25 km/h. Water volume ranges from 60 cu.m/sec. to 600 cu.m/sec. (20,000 cfs). For about 12 km the river is a steady grade 2. Then Chilcotin Canyon is reached, several kilometres of very fast water, flanked by towering cliffs and often in shadow. Rapids reach grade 3 generally. Then a dead flat pool in the river and a hush of silence until building in the distance comes a roar like a railway. Pull out here to scout Railroad Rapid, following a flagged trail on the right bank. This rapid was formed in 1972/73 when a hugh slide tumbled down the north canyon wall. Although it may wash out in years to come it is now a grade 5 to 6. It is almost impossible to portage or line because of the steep cliffs and continuous skree slopes that form the canyon. Large inflatables have negotiated this rapid, but even 18 footers have folded up like paper boats in the haystacks, spewing boaters into the cold water. It **may** be possible in a kayak, but no reports are available.

Below the Railroad Rapid the river remains confined for a kilometre or two and then breaks out in the open approach to the Fraser. A final grade 3 rapid, the Caboose, sometimes drowned out in high water, brings paddlers to the Fraser. There is no vehicle access to this point, and although you may notice a road going up the south bank it is not passable even to a four-wheel drive. The only practical egress is to follow the Fraser south from 106 km, another 26 kilometres to the Gang Ranch Bridge, where it is possible rendezvous with a vehicle and pull out on the left bank below the bridge.

If you have paddled the Chilcotin Canyon the Fraser should not present any problems but remember that it is a high volume flow and paddlers should have grade 3 experience. The river is 100 metres wide here with a minimum flow of 350 cubic metres per second, making boils and whirlpools common. The take-out point at the Gang Ranch bridge is reached from the Cariboo Highway near Clinton or south from Williams Lake on the Dog Creek Road.

ROUTE - TURNER LAKE CHAIN - TWEEDSMUIR PARK
GRADE - *Lake with 1-2 between*
LENGTH - *36 km return*
WIDTH - *varies*
VERTICAL DROP - *Approximately 122 metres*
TIME TO ALLOW - *1 week*
NEAREST EMERGENCY COMMUNICATION - *Hunlen Wilderness Camp or Highway 20*
CAMPING - ACCOMMODATION - *Cleared sites on lakes*
MAPS - *N.T.S 1:50,000 93C/4E&W; 1:250,000 93C Anahim*
HAZARDS - *Rock gardens on creeks, remote*

DIRECTIONS

The Turner Lake Chain is reached by flying in from Williams Lake or Nimpo Lake, or walking a trail from Highway 20 up the Atnarko River to Turner Lake. The latter is not recommended for canoeists.

DESCRIPTION

The Turner Lake Chain lies in the southern part of Tweedsmuir Park. They lie along Hunlen Creek, a tributary of the Atnarko River in the area of Lonesome Lake, the area made popular by Ralph Edwards, the Crusoe of Lonesome Lake. The chain consists of six lakes: Turner, Hunlen, Vista, Junker, Widgeon and Kidney, connected by Hunlen Creek. Nestled in the coast mountains, the lakes are surrounded by heavy forest with mountains and glaciers looming in the distance. Mosquitoes are numerous but fishing is good for cutthroat trout, planted years ago by the Edwards.

There are cleared campsites with pit toilets on each of the lakes. Sandy beaches also make good stopping points. The creek between the lakes can sometimes be lined and waded, though this is often difficult. Portages are more practical in some areas. There is a 1 km portage between Turner and Hunlen and another difficult steep climb into Kidney Lake, the final one of the chain.

The creeks can be hard on canoes so it is suggested that paddlers make their access easier by renting canoes from John Edwards, at Hunlen Wilderness Camp on Turner Lake, reached via the Bella Coola post office. Some staples can be purchased here and a few supplies are rented. Wilderness Airways in Williams Lake can be contacted about fly-in arrangements.

Other points of interest in the area include the original Edwards homestead, reached via a long steep trail from Turner Lake. The elevation drop is 760 metres. If you use the trail please respect these people's privacy. At the far end of Turner Lake Hunlen Creek drops off the plateau, forming 260 metre Hunlen Falls, now accessible by a new trail that reaches the Atnarko River.

ROUTE - BELLA COOLA RIVER *Natural River*
LENGTH - *Approx. 65 km*
WIDTH - *n/a*
VERTICAL DROP - *Approximately 150 metres*
TIME TO ALLOW - *1 to 2 days*
NEAREST EMERGENCY COMMUNICATION - *Hagensborg or Bella Coola*
CAMPING - ACCOMMODATION - *Provincial campgrounds at Atnarko, 69 km east of Bella Coola and Burnt Bridge, 43 km east of Bella Coola*
MAPS - *N.T.S. 1:250,000 93D Bella Coola*
HAZARDS - *Log jam, sweepers*

DIRECTIONS

Travel west from Williams on Highway 20, a gravel road. Put-in at Burnt Bridge or below Firvale to avoid a log jam. Take-out at Bella Coola.

DESCRIPTION

Limited information was available on this route so canoeists should be prepared to scout it out thoroughly before embarking. It is canoeable but the upper section could present some log jam hazards. A large jam is reported at Firvale and it might be easier to launch below this.

MacKenzie canoed this section with natives in large sea going canoes at the end of his transcontinental journey in 1793. Up Thorsen Creek, near the outskirts of Bella Coola, there are petroglyphs carved in the rocks and along the river itself are numerous archeological sites. The river takes its name from the local Indians.

This route is through the Coastal Forest biotic zone and rain can be expected. The dominent vegetation is cedar, hemlock and Douglas fir, and the typical heavy undergrowth that makes coastal land travel so difficult.

ROUTE - WEST ROAD RIVER [BLACKWATER] *Natural River*
GRADE - *1 to 3*
LENGTH - *Approximately 260 km, 15 to 22 portages*
WIDTH - *3 to 30 metres*
VERTICAL DROP - *396 metres; 1.5 metres per km*
TIME TO ALLOW - *10 days*
NEAREST EMERGENCY COMMUNICATION - *Quesnel, 300 km from put-in. There is a lodge on Tsacha and a ranch on Euchiniko Lakes*
CAMPING - ACCOMMODATION - *Unorganized*
MAPS - *N.T.S. 1:250,000 93C Anahim; 93F Nechako River; 93G Prince George*
HAZARDS - *Remote wilderness, rapids, waterfalls*

DIRECTIONS

Fly-in to Eliguk Lake, highest access point, or Tsacha Lake, 40 km downstream. Four-wheel drive can sometimes reach Euchiniko Lakes, approximately 75 km downstream. Take-out at Lower Blackwater Crossing. Below this is a dangerous impassable canyon. Float planes can be chartered in Quesnel, Williams Lake or Nimpo Lake. Some reports say that four-wheel drive can reach Eliguk via Anahim Lake and the Dean River.

The West Road, or Blackwater, trip is a fairly difficult, arduous trip, and should not be attempted except by experienced wilderness paddlers. During the 260 kilometre paddle there will be between 15 and 22 portages, food will have to be carried for 10 days, and there is no emergency communication except a few Indians with wagons, some scattered ranches and perhaps passing aircraft. Paddlers should be in good condition and well supplied with emergency gear. This remoteness is what makes the West Road trip attractive to those looking for a challenging paddle.

For the most part the trip follows the route taken by Alexander Mackenzie when he first crossed to the Pacific Ocean in July of 1793, for although he did not canoe the river he did have to wade it many times. Mackenzie was following a route used by the native people for centuries as a means of connecting the Fraser River to the ocean at Bella Coola. They told him that the river was navigable to the Fraser except for two rapids. Mackenzie named the river the West Road, now the official name, though it became known locally as the Blackwater. It was into this country that Rich Hobson and Pan Phillips rode to start their cattle ranches, an enterprise that resulted in Hobson writing two books on the area, *Grass Beyond the Mountains* and *Nothing Too Good For a Cowboy*. A later book by Hillan, *Blackwater River*, would also be good reading for those interested in this trip.

The West Road River rises at the north end of the Ilgachuz Range, almost due north of the Chilcotin country's Anahim Lake. The 900 metre peaks of the Ilgachuz Range are extinct volcanoes, formed into the classical conical shape. From there the river flows 300 kilometres west, between the Fraser and Nechako Plateaus, crossing the Telegraph Range to join the Fraser River near Quesnel. The valley of the West Road is in the Cariboo Parkland biotic zone or Montane forest region, characterized by a mixture of grasslands, deciduous groves and light forest with lodgepole pine and Douglas fir, often called cattle country.

Wildlife includes cariboo, moose mule deer, black bear, grizzly bear, wold, coyote, beaver and numerous other fur-bearers such as fisher, marten, otter, mink and wolverine. Birds likely to be seen are eagles, osprey, terns, jays, songbirds, Canada geese, mergansers and ducks. Fishing is good on most of the system and superb on the headwaters. Eliguk Lake for instance has spectacular fly fishing for 10 to 20 kilogram rainbows. There are also lake trout, Dolly Varden and kokanee. Salmon migrate in May and June but are illegal to catch.

The place to start if you wish to canoe the complete river is Eliguk Lake, 5 kilometres long, which drains into Ulgato Creek. This first section of river requires difficult portaging and lining, with shallow water and few campsites. Ulgato Creek is too shallow to canoe so portage along a wagon road on the left. Put-in again at a small lake. Soon the West Road flows in from the south, though the river is still very shallow and narrow. This section may have to be lined as after 8 km a rocky section is reached where the depth is only 5 to 20 centimetres. Twenty km from Eliguk Lake, Carnlick Creek flows in from the south, its cooler, green water increasing the depth and velocity. The headwaters of Carnlick Creek is where Hobson and Phillips established their Home Ranch.

One and a half kilometres below the creek is a farm operation and after a similar distance rock gardens stretch 4 km to two small falls. Portage on the right. More rock gardens and a chute follow. On the next section the river drops steeply with numerous large rocks on the river bed. Two more rapids both require portaging, the first on the left shore, the second on the right. Shortly a 1000 metre canyon appears, flanked by 65 metre basalt walls. The canyon ends in a 15 metre waterfall. Portage on the right. Below the falls are three impassable ledges, bypassed by hauling along the right shore 400 metres. Below the ledges.is a 200 metre rapid. Beyond these obstructions the river meanders 6.5 km to Tsacha Lake.

Tsacha and Euchiniko Lakes make a 55 km section of lake grade water, joined by grade 2 to 3 water, and a waterfall. Tsacha Lake is 20 km long, surrounded by hills and mountains. There is a lodge on this lake. At the east end watch for a cabin that marks the beginning of a series of rapids. Portage along the right. A short paddle follows and then a series of six ledges, best portaged 450 metres along the right. Four chutes are then encountered, a short series of rapids and a 4 metre waterfall, passed with a 200 metre carry along the right bank. Two more rapids below the falls can be run after scouting. A short meander leads to Euchiniko Lakes.

Euchiniko Lake is 30 km long, narrow, with a riverlike character, and bordered by open slopes reaching 1000 metres in height. Some weedy shallows can make paddling difficult. About one quarter of the way along the right shore of the second lake a river flows in from Kluskus Lakes. Portaging or lining about 2 km up this river would give canoeists access to another 15 km of paddling, 30 return, on the Kluskus Lakes. Mackenzie travelled along the northern shore of these lakes during his trek and the

partially abandoned village of Kluskus still stands near the junction of the two lakes. The Euchiniko Ranch offers some services to wilderness travellers.

The 80 km segment from Euchiniko Lakes to Euchiniko River consists of shallow rock gardens, frequent braiding of channels and low river banks. The first section to Kluskoil Lake is difficult but no portages are necessary as rock gardens are shallow enough to allow walking or lining around impassable areas.

Camping on Kluskoil Lake is best along the open left shore. Past the lake is a series of falls and ledges. Portage 100 metres along the left shore for 400 metres, using part of the wagon road. More rock gardens require walking or lining.

Soon the confluence with the Nazko River is approached. A bridge just upstream could be a pull-out. The bridge is on the Nazko road which connects the village of Nazko, to the south, to Quesnel. The influence of the Nazko broadens the West Road; braiding is more common on a wide flood plain. There are no rapids. More traffic is seen along the river in this section with many campers and fishermen using the Blackwater road for river access.

At the confluence of the Euchiniko River the West Road increases to 6.5 km per hour and narrows to an average of 25 metres, with a gradient of 10 metres per mile. Paddlers not experienced in whitewater may wish to pull out by finding convenient road access near the confluence, or by paddling up the Euchiniko a short distance to a bridge. Several large dangerous rapids are downstream between here and the Lower Blackwater Bridge. Depending on water levels some can be run while others will have to be portaged. Downstream 13 km the river enters a small canyon 8 km long, filled with chutes, ledges and rapids. The river is fast and steep. At about 25 km another canyon is entered, prefaced by two violent rapids. The canyon is 100 metres deep with a width of only 15 metres. It must be scouted. There is an 800 metre portage on the left that will bypass the canyon. Another 15 km, around some sharp bends, then a sharp left and the Lower Blackwater bridge can be seen. Do not miss this take-out. Below is the lower canyon of the West Road, impassable and dangerous. To reach Quesnel take the road south, to the right.

ROUTE - BOWRON LAKE CHAIN - BOWRON PARK
GRADE - *Lake and grade 2*
LENGTH - *116 km, 6 portages*
WIDTH - *Up to 2.5 km*
VERTICAL DROP - *52 metres*
TIME TO ALLOW - *7 to 10 days*
NEAREST EMERGENCY COMMUNICATION - *Park Headquarters or Wells 29 km*
CAMPING - ACCOMMODATION - *Accommodation in Quesnel or Wells. Camping at designated sites on chain*

MAPS - *Dept. of Lands and Forests 1:63,360, Bowron Lake Park*
HAZARDS - *Some wind and fast water, wilderness*

DIRECTIONS

From Quesnel on Highway 97 drive east 112 km to Park. Trip begins with a portage from near campground and ends at Bowron Lake.

DESCRIPTION

The Bowron Lake Chain is one of the oldest and most popular recreational canoe areas in British Columbia. More has been written on this area than any other canoe area, probably in North America. Consequently it is crowded in summer months and loses some of the wilderness appeal it once had.

To write more on this chain seems to be redundant. Parks branch have excellent descriptive brochures which detail the route around the circuit. With this brochure and a good map little other information is needed. Canoeists should however have some canoe experience and particularly experience in wilderness travel. For this reason we will not detail the route here but rather give the reader enough information to understand the area and the route.

Bowron Lake Provincial Park in the Cariboo Mountains is a wilderness region of more than 121 600 hectares, an area roughly rectangular in shape. It forms a canoe circuit of six lakes and connecting waterways. The park and lake are named for John Bowron, one of the Overlanders of 1862 who came to the Cariboo in search of gold. He was one of the few who settled here, becoming one of the leading civil servants of the region.

The circuit is surrounded by rugged mountains, averaging about 2 100 metres in elevation, that form a scenic backdrop for a magnificent wildlife sanctuary. Moose are the most frequently seen, often feeding in the shallow marshes along lakes and river courses. Closed to hunting the area is also a popular one with bears and campers should be sure to check with park's staff as to what precautions are best. Caribou, and mountain goat inhabit the high country along with grizzly bears, which sometimes come down to lakeshore. In fall they frequent the Bowron River in large numbers, feeding on the spawning salmon.

Upon arriving in the park visitors must register at the Information Centre before taking the circuit, and must check out on return. Parks Branch warns that canoeists should come well prepared and well equipped as this is a wilderness region with no services anywhere on the circuit. Camping is confined to designated areas and all garbage must be carried out. All domestic pets are prohibited and wild animals must not of course be fed.

In an effort to preserve the wilderness atmosphere of the park the size of groups has been restricted. Except on Bowron Lake itself, groups must not exceed six persons. Groups exceeding six persons will be required to separate into parties of six persons or less before proceeding. Departure of sections may be delayed up to 48 hours to ensure that sections do not join up while on the circuit.

The circuit is made in a clockwise direction and begins with the hardest portage, 2.4 km from the campground to Kibbee Creek. This leads to small Kibbee Lake and then a 2 km portage to Indianpoint Lake, 4 km long. Then there is a portage of less than 1 km to Isaac Lake. Isaac Lake is 32 km long. Most canoeists follow the outside of this lake, the safest and most interesting route. The lake is emptied by the Isaac River which leads to McLeary Lake. This is 2.8 km in length but some of the river will have to be portaged. How much will depend on the skill of the paddler. Do not over estimate your skill as more than one canoe has got into difficulty here. There is a log jam and falls at the end of the river that will also have to be portaged. McLeary Lake is only 1.2 km long.

From here the Cariboo River flows 5.2 km to Lanezi Lake, 14.8 km long, and then 1.2 km to Sandy Lake, 4.8 km long. Lanezi Lake has few places to land so it is not advisable to travel if the wind is blowing. Watch for sweepers and snags in the river sections.

From Sandy Lake the Cariboo River is followed for 3.6 km to Babcock Creek although an interesting side trip is to head into Unna Lake and hike to Cariboo Falls. Babcock Creek is lined to Babcock Lake, a distance of 1.2 km. Babcock Lake is 2.8 km in length and then a portage leads 0.4 of a km to Skoi Lake. Skoi Lake is less than a kilometre in length and then there is a final short portage to Spectacle Lakes. These are just under 13 km in length. From there the route winds through a marsh area leading toward Bowron Lake. This is a particularly good place to watch for moose. The Bowron River is 4 km and after that there remains only Bowron Lake, 7.2 km in length and you are back at the campsite.

ROUTE - CARIBOO RIVER

GRADE - *2 to 3, rapids to 5*

LENGTH - *76 km, 4 portages on Cariboo; 30 km, 2 portages on Bowron chain*

WIDTH - *50 metres*

VERTICAL DROP - *238 metres*

TIME TO ALLOW - *4 to 5 days*

NEAREST EMERGENCY COMMUNICATION - *Keithly Creek on Cariboo Lake, Likely on Quesnel Lake*

CAMPING - ACCOMMODATION - *Unorganized along route. Campsite on Unna Lake at beginning of trip*

MAPS - *N.T.S 1:250,000 93H McBride; 93A Quesnel Lake; and/or Dept. Lands & Forests 1:63,360 Bowron Lake Park; Pre-emptor series, Quesnel sheet*

HAZARDS - *Wilderness, waterfalls, grade 5 rapids, log drives on river*

DIRECTIONS

From Quesnel on Highway 97 drive to Bowron Lake Park and canoe the last portion of the circuit in reverse, through Bowron Lake to Unna Lake, 30 km. The Cariboo river begins here. Take-out at Quesnel Forks, or follow Quesnel River route to Quesnel.

DESCRIPTION

This river is not for novices. There are several rapids and 2 waterfalls that must be portaged. Water volume is estimated at 1200 to 1700 cu.m/sec. and the gradient at 3 m/km.

The headwaters of the Cariboo River are in the ice-fields of the Cariboo Mountains. From there the river flows across and through the Quesnel Highlands, part of the Fraser Plateau. Along the river there is much evidence of the glacial action that formed this part of the province, in fact the starting point of Unna Lake is a large kettle hole in the outwash plain of a glacier.

Dominent trees of this region are Douglas Fir, spruce, lodgepole pine and some aspen thickets along the banks. Down river the deciduous growth increases. Wildlife most often seen is moose, black bear, and some grizzly, mule deer, beaver, otter, coyote, wolf, weasel and porcupine. Bird life varies and larger birds tend to be more easily recorded, therefore eagles, osprey and hawks are the most commonly seen. Dolly Varden, lake trout and rainbow are found in the waters but logging operations and the floating of logs in the river has adversely affected fish stocks.

The history of this region is tied closely to the discovery of gold, for before that few men had entered this region. Keithly Creek, on Cariboo Lake was the site of a gold strike in 1859 and soon men had crossed the mountains to the Barkerville region to find the mother lode. Quesnel Forks at the routes terminus was for a time the capital of B.C. and was an important stopping place on the trail to Cariboo. Now all that remains of these strikes are a few cabins, and a few people still hoping to find a new eldorado. Paddlers might like to take a gold pan along and try washing for gold on the rivers gravel bars.

Paddlers wanting to travel the complete river will have to start by following 30 km of the Bowron circuit in reverse, heading south to Unna Lake. An alternative is to fly into Kimball Lake, about 16 km downriver. Downstream from Unna Lake just a kilometer and one half is Cariboo Falls. A small rapid just upstream of the falls can be run by keeping right. The portage is on the right bank beginning about 20 metres upstream of the 25 metre drop. Don't miss it. The portage is 750 metres long and in poor condition. It ends at a trapper's cabin. Below the falls the river has three mild rapids that can be run. A larger rapid 8 km below the falls indicates the beginning of a gorge which cannot be run. It is 3 km in length and located just above Kimball Lake near where Limestone Creek flows in from the north. An old logging road on the right serves as a rough portage, 5 km in length with a climb of 395 metres.

Kimball Lake is really a 2 km widening of the river. From here the river meanders for 24 km to Cariboo Lake, 15 km long. The settlement of Keithly Creek is near the south end, on a penninsula of land that narrows the lake.

Five km downstream of Cariboo Lake there are three wide rapids that precede a waterfall. Near here logs are dumped into the lake so they now present an added hazard, particularly while running whitewater. There is no trail around the falls so either side can be used for a 100 metre carry. Below the falls the river is swift and narrow for 3 km, past Sellar Creek. Below this fast section is another canyon with grade 5 water that must be portaged. Carry 500 metres on the left side. Downstream of this canyon the water is swift and difficult but navigable. About 5 km below Sellars Creek, the river is bridged by the road from Likely to Keithly Creek. Just upstream Spanish Creek flows in on the left.

The first 5 km below the bridge consists of large standing waves and big holes. This section must be run with extreme caution as most of the eddies have been blocked with floating booms to prevent log jams. This allows no place for a rest or pull-out in case of an upset. Past Murderer's Gulch the river begins to widen with quick bouncy rapids that are not difficult to run. Some bends will have large standing waves on the outside that can be avoided. As the river swings to the south buildings will be noticed on the left bank and the remains of an old ferry crossing on the right. This is Quesnel Forks, first surveyed by the Royal Engineers in 1861 and the site of many fine old buildings. Unfortunately many have disappeared in the river as the banks eroded away. This is the terminus of the Cariboo River. A road from Quesnel Forks connects with the main road to Likely and Williams Lake. The trip can be continued down the Quesnel River to Quesnel.

ROUTE - QUESNEL RIVER *Recreational River*
GRADE - *2, with rapids to 5*
LENGTH - *104 km, 3 portages*
WIDTH - *50 metres*
VERTICAL DROP - *224 metres*
TIME TO ALLOW - *3 days*
NEAREST EMERGENCY COMMUNICATION - *Likely and Quesnel*
CAMPING - ACCOMMODATION - *Unorganized*
MAPS - *N.T.S 1:250,000 93A Quesnel Lake; 93B Quesnel; 93G Prince George. Dept. of Lands and Forests Pre-emptor series, Quesnel sheet*
HAZARDS - *Log drives, rapids to grade 5, wilderness*

DIRECTIONS

From Williams Lake drive to Likely. Rafters and kayakers may put in here if expert. Canoeists are best to put in at Quesnel Forks. Take-out point is the town of Quesnel.

DESCRIPTION

Although generally rated at grade 2 this river has some very difficult sections, and some which must be portaged. It should not be attempted by those not in good condition and unprepared to portage. The first section from Likely to Quesnel Forks is not recommended for open canoes but is included for kayakers or whitewater rafters. A road from Likely leads to Quesnel Forks.

The Quesnel River was one of the major rivers of the Cariboo goldrush of the early 1860's. Near here was the town of Bullion where Dancing Bill Latham made a strike in 1859. In later years the Cariboo Hydraulic Mining Company was formed and by hydraulicing the river banks took out millions of dollars worth of gold. Likely was the site of gold strikes too. It was first known as Quesnel Dam but later was renamed after "Plato John" Likely, a miner who lectured on the ancient philosophers, and who found a lot of gold in the area. A guide to the history and points of interest of this area is *Cariboo Mileposts,* by the authors of this book and published by Mitchell Press.

From Likely the river is extremely fast, first passing under the bridge to Williams Lake and then dropping into a small clogged rock canyon. Water volumes in late summer were approximately 2900 cu.m/sec. to 3400

cu.m/sec. The gradient is approximately 6.5 metres/km with many large standing and moving waves. At 5 km Bullion Pool is reached, the area hydrauliced by the mine at Bullion Camp. There is a large eddy here.

The next 7 km drops even faster, dropping into a rock clogged canyon of grade 5+, nearly a km in length. This area is known by locals as the "Devil's Eyebrow". Just below the canyon is a rock ledge that creates a large hole that should be avoided. One km downstream, the clear Quesnel joins the bark laden Cariboo and the log drives of lumber companies.

Below Quesnel Forks the water volume increases with addition of the flow from the Cariboo River. Generally though the river is wide and easy for many miles. Hazards in this section are limited to the occasional sand bar and sweeper, and the booms and logs of lumber companies. Jet boats may use the river from time to time during log drives.

Just upstream of Buxton Creek the river has some tight bends with high banks and fast water producing standing waves, boils and whirlpools. 1.5 km downstream from the mouth of Beaver Creek there is a large rapid. This is marked on the old pre-emptor series but not the newer series. Run this one along the left shore. Another 8 km and there is a strong S-shaped chute, just below a small island. At some water levels this may be run but a portage can also be made along the right shore. From here there is little problem as far as the bridge at Sardine Flats. Be careful of the log booms here. Canoeists who do not want to portage the next two canyons should take-out here. This was once the side of the Gravelle Ferry. The road will lead north to Quesnel.

Eight km below the bridge the river enters a short rapid called Little Canyon. The pre-emptor series maps mark it as being capable of producing 52,800 horsepower, the same as Big Canyon further downstream. The canyon below Likely though, shows as producing 78,300 horse power. This canyon can be portaged or run on the left between the boils and the standing waves. Just below is another chute to run, on the left again.

Now the river flows for 10 km to Big Canyon. This is impassable for anything except inflatables with an experienced crew. The canyon is 5 km long. Approach on the right shore and portage along a road seen from the river. In the canyon large boulders create enormous hydraulics creating giant boils, holes and drops. It is not a good place for open canoes.

Below Big Canyon the river loops to the south and passes the town of Quesnel and then joins the Fraser River. A good take-out point is the Riverside Motel.

The river was named for Jules Maurice Quesnel, a clerk of the North West Company who was 22 years old when he passed here with Simon Fraser. In his journal for Monday August 1st 1808 Fraser writes; "Set out early. Debarked at Quesnel's River where we found some of the natives, from whom we procured some furs, plenty of fish and berries. Continued our route until sunset."

For many years the town that grew here during the gold rush was referred to as Quesnelle Mouth, to distinguish it from Quesnelle Forks, but in the early 1900's the post office changed and shortened the name.

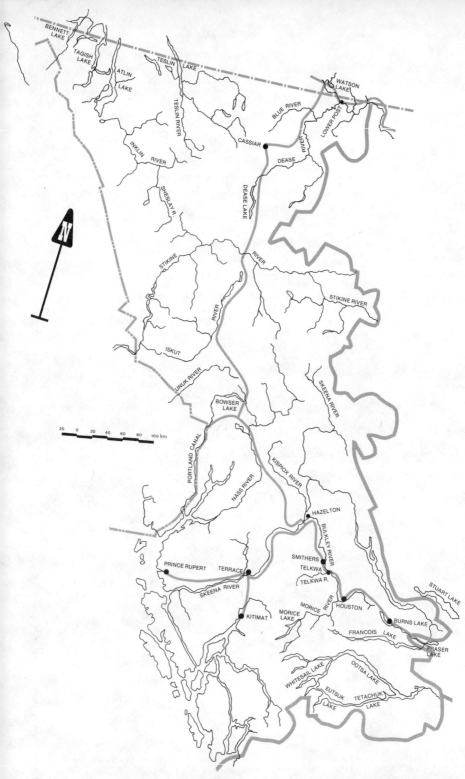

SKEENA REGION

ROUTE - BULKLEY RIVER - HOUSTON TO SMITHERS
GRADE - *1 with rapids to 2*
LENGTH - *80 km*
WIDTH - *20 to 50 metres*
VERTICAL DROP - *Approximately 120 metres, 1.5 metres per km*
TIME TO ALLOW - *One day or more*
NEAREST EMERGENCY COMMUNICATION - *Houston, Quick Bridge, Telkwa, Smithers*
CAMPING - ACCOMMODATION - *Campside at Houston put-in or unorganized along route. Accommodation in Houston and Smithers*
MAPS - *N.T.S 1:50,000 93L/7 E&W Houston; 93L/10W Quick; 93L/11 E Telkwa; 93L/14 E Smithers*
HAZARDS - *Deadheads and some fast water*

DIRECTIONS

On Highway 16 about 2 km west of Houston a bridge crosses the Bulkley River. On the upstream side, left bank, there is a picnic and camping area provided by a timber company. Put-in here.

DESCRIPTION

This pleasant trip follows the route of the Bulkley Valley Fall Fair canoe race, a popular annual event that almost any class of paddler can enter. The race actually starts downstream at the Barrett Bridge. The Bulkley is a fairly quiet run except for a chute just upstream of Telkwa and a few others between there and Smithers. These could be grade 2 depending on the water levels. The only other hazards are a few deadheads and as on all rivers the possibility of sweepers.

The volume of water seen at the launching point is not indicative of the Bulkley for just downstream the much larger flow of the Morice enters. Father Morice, after whom the river is named, was a priest, historian and cartographer of the north. On his early maps he more accurately had the smaller stream named the Morice, with the Bulkley continuing upstream to Loring Lake, now Morice Lake. A later cartographer, Poudrier, apparently without ever seeing the two streams confused the two names, causing the incongruity that exists today.

In future years water volumes at this confluence may again alter. The proposed Kemano II project plans to reverse the flow on the Nanika River, which provides 40% of the Morice flow. This would probably mean the end of the spring and coho salmon runs that are so popular with anglers. The river is also heavily fished for steelhead from September to March.

Down river from the confluence paddlers will pass Barrett Bridge and Ranch, the former ranch of Charlie Barrett an early packer of the Bulkley

Valley. Then Walcott, once a town and station on the Grand Trunk Pacific and now just a few buildings and a foot bridge, is passed on the left bank. Watch for deer, beaver, red-necked grebes, sandhill cranes in the fall, and other birds.

Plan on stopping at Paddon's General Store at Quick as an opportunity to stretch your legs. This is one of the most unique structures in the province. The rambling building began in 1922 and was gradually added to as the need for space increased. One end of the store was added in payment of a debt. For a time a small town grew up at the Station of Quick, named for a section foreman, but as the road took business away from the railway it became less economical to maintain. In 1965 the station and other buildings were torn down. Only the general store remains.

A few kilometres downstream a large clearing will be seen on the left side of the river. This was once the site of Hubert, a fledgling town that promotors hoped would be the divisional point of the G.T.P. It was passed up in favor of Smithers.

Telkwa, another few kilometres downstream, likewise hoped to be the divisional point. Unlike Hubert is refused to die. In 1977 the old hotel burned down so don't count on a meal break here. Canoeists will pass a large rock at the junction of the Bulkley and Telkwa Rivers that was once featured in Ripley's *Believe It or Not* as being the only rock in the world with three major bridges leaving it. At present there are only two, although the pilings of the third can be seen.

From Telkwa downstream there are a few fast stretches of water but they should not present any problem for reasonably experienced canoeists. Soon Smithers is reached, or at least the bridge above Smithers. Pull-out near the Highway 16 bridge. There is a short steep bank here. The trip could be terminated earlier, at Telkwa, where road access is easy.

ROUTE - KISPIOX RIVER
GRADE - *2 +*
LENGTH - *65 km*
WIDTH - *25 metres*
VERTICAL DROP - *150 metres; 2.3 metres per km*
TIME TO ALLOW - *2 days*
NEAREST EMERGENCY COMMUNICATION - *Lodges on river or Hazelton*
CAMPING - ACCOMMODATION - *B.C.F.S. campsite at Mile 20*
MAPS - *N.T.S. 1:250,000 103P Nass River; 93M Hazelton*
HAZARDS - *Some logs and deadheads. One log jam*

DIRECTIONS

Take Highway 16 to Hazelton. From Hazelton take road to Kispiox, then follow the road along the east side of the Kispiox River to Sweetin River. Put-in here, take-out at Kispiox village bridge.

DESCRIPTION

The Kispiox is a mellow river in a spectacular setting, with mountains in the background and historic Indian villages to visit. Along the route canoeists will see mergansers, red-necked grebes, perhaps a black bear or grizzly if salmon are spawning, and beaver. In fall sandhill cranes pass through and they may be heard passing overhead or seen feeding in fields. The fishing is excellent, particularly for steelhead. A cautionary note though: Angling from boats is not permitted on the Kispiox River. Check your fishing regulations.

Near the beginning of the trip there may be a log jam that will have to be portaged. Further down there is a small canyon with some tricky water half way between Sportsman Lodge and the Kispiox Bridge. Other than these two spots the river is unremarkable and should present no problems.

There are three lodges along the river: Kispiox Steelhead Camp; Sportsman's Kispiox Lodge, 26 km from Hazelton; and Raven Wood resort, 35 km from Hazelton. Accommodation and some supplies are available at all of these lodges.

There is an Indian village with some fine totems at the junction of the Kispiox with the Skeena, and a replica village at K'san that should be visited by anyone travelling to this area.

ROUTE - DEASE RIVER *Wild River*
GRADE - *2*
LENGTH - *265 km*
WIDTH - *15 to 35 metres*
VERTICAL DROP - *Approximately 150 metres; 5 decimetres per km*
TIME TO ALLOW - *1 week*
NEAREST EMERGENCY COMMUNICATION - *Stewart Cassiar Highway at Dease Lake or Lower Post at terminus. Lodge on Cotton Lake*
CAMPING - ACCOMMODATION - *Unorganized on route. Boya Lake Park 85 km south of Watson Lake, 35 campsites. Lodge on Cotton Lake*
MAPS - *N.T.S. 1:250,000 104J Dease Lake; 104I Cry Lake; 104P McDame*
HAZARDS - *Some log jams, grade 3 rapids, remote*

DIRECTIONS

Access to Dease Lake is from either Watson Lake, Y.T. on the Alaska Highway, 225 km north or from the Stewart Cassiar Highway. Stewart is 320 km south. It would also be possible to fly in to Dease Lake by float plane from Watson Lake. Take-out is at Lower Post, across the Liard River and easily reached from the Alaska Highway.

DESCRIPTION

The Dease River is likely to become one of the most popular canoe routes in the province, for it combines wilderness, history, interesting flora and fauna and an interesting landscape with 265 km of fairly easy canoeing.

Historically it has been an important route to link the ocean, via the Stikine River, to the Cassiar and Yukon country. As early as 1834 John McLeod of the H.B.C. came along this valley as far as the Tuya River, and in 1838 Robert Campbell made a smiliar journey. The following year the first trading post was built on Sawmill Point in Dease Lake. The lake and river were named by McLeod in 1834 for Peter Warren Dease, at that time in charge of New Caledonia and stationed at Fort St. James. When gold was discovered at McDame traffic increased, and then a veritable rush came through during the Klondike years. Following that it was one of the few routes to the northern interior, and as a route for barges and scows served to carry supplies north for the building of the Alaska Highway during World War II. Two books, *Campbell of the Yukon* by Clifford Wilson and *Trail to the Interior* by R.M. Patterson give a good account of the history and people of the Dease.

The south end of Dease Lake lies practically on the divide between the Pacific and Artic drainages. Just 3 km south is the Tanzilla River which flows south to join the Stikine. From the Dease all waters flow north. The Dease River flows gently through the Cassiar Mountains and then across the Liard Plain to the Liard River near Lower Post. Most of the river bed is cut through glacial till, passing some swampy areas of poor drainage until it cuts down to bed rock at the Two and Four Mile Rapids near the Liard.

Spruce and poplar form the dominant tree cover with willow and alder along the shore. On the hills above are alpine forests and open meadows.

Moose are frequently seen along the river or nearby lakes. Black bear, grizzly, wolf, lynx, fox, beaver, marmot and chipmunks are also seen. High on the nearby mountains are stone sheep and mountain goats and a few caribou. Like on most rivers, mergansers and geese are often sighted along with loons, gulls, bald eagles, nighthawks, great-horned owls, ptarmigan, whiskey jacks, ravens, sandpipers, kingfisher and waxwings. Fishing in the Arctic drainage offers a chance to catch grayling, one of the most beautiful of sport fish. Lakes contain lake trout, rainbow and Dollies.

The canoe trip begins at the southern end of Dease Lake, 45 km in length but quite narrow. The group of buildings on the south shore were once known as Lakehouse. Dease Landing is a few kilometres up the east side; Laketon lies near the mouth of Dease Creek on the west shore; Porter Landing is on the west shore near the end of the lake; and the old H.B.C. post was on Sawmill Point, on the east side just south of the lakes end. All of these places are worth a visit by the canoeist. They are all described in Bruce Ramsey's *Ghost Towns of British Columbia*.

From the end of the lake the river flows in a north-east direction with a speed of about 4 km per hour. The depth from here to Joe Irwin Lake, a widening of the river, is about 1.2 metres. Watch for a few log jams. A series of lakes are passed, first Anvil, then Joe Irwin, Pine Tree and Cotton Lakes. The lakes vary from 2 to 6 km in length. They are shallow with bushy shorelines, dominated by a fine view of the Cassiar Mountains. One set of rapids occurs just below Pine Tree Lake but they comprise just a few riffles with standing waves in midstream, easily passed with a canoe. There is a lodge on Cotton Lake.

Just past the Cottonwood River are two sets of small rapids, Cottonwood and Stone Island Rapid. There are small standing waves and some boulders to be avoided but they are easily navigated.

Where McDame Creek flows in from the west a few buildings mark the site of McDame, an abandoned H.B.C. post. The area was first known as Sylvester's Landing, for in 1876 Rufus Sylvester built a trading post here hoping to cash in on the miners who were coming for gold. Later the post was bought by H.B.C. This is approximately half way on the journey.

When the Blue River flows in, again from the west, the current quickens to 6.5 km per hour. The river widens and the velocity causes more cut banks. The Four Mile rapids are named for their distance from the Liard and unlike the earlier easy rapids, can be dangerous and should be scouted. There are large standing waves on the left and shallows on the right, divided by a small island. Take the right, watching for rocks in the shallow water. Two Mile Rapids are next, and last. They occur as the river narrows and sweeps around a right bend. Some jagged rocks are in the centre of the channel. Stay right, on the inside of the turn. Shortly the Liard River will be seen. Lower Post is directly across the Liard opposite a small island at the mouth of the Dease. Paddle or line upstream to the far end of the island and then paddle across the Liard. The town is on the Alaska Highway and has telephone, supplies and accommodation.

ROUTE - STIKINE RIVER *Wild River*
GRADE - *2 to 3, rapids to 6*
LENGTH - *459 km, plus Grand Canyon, 80 km; 3 to 5 portages*
WIDTH - *10 to 250 metres*
VERTICAL DROP - *1296 metres; 2.8 metres per km*
TIME TO ALLOW - *2 weeks*
NEAREST EMERGENCY COMMUNICATION - *Telegraph Creek; outfitters camp near Spatsizi River and Cassiar Highway crossing*
CAMPING - ACCOMMODATION - *Unorganized*
MAPS - *N.T.S. 1:250,000 104H Spatsizi; 94E Toodoggone River; 104I Cry Lake; 104J Dease Lake; 104G Telegraph Creek; 104B Iskut River*
HAZARDS - *Remote, rapids, canyon*

DIRECTIONS

Fly-in from Watson Lake to Tuaton Lake on the Stikine headwaters. Take-out at Cassiar Highway and portage to Telegraph Creek. Take-out on lower Stikine by float plane or river barge, or continue another 65 km to Wrangell, Alaska.

DESCRIPTION

This lengthy canoe journey down one of the largest of B.C.'s rivers starts at the very headwaters of the stream, Tuaton Lake, 1926 metres high in the Cassiar Mountains. From there is cuts its way through the Spatsizi Plateau until it is bounded on the north by the Stikine Range. With the exception of the Grand Canyon section the valley is wide, always forming the demarcation between various mountain ranges, offering spectacular views and vistas.

At the headwaters the country is like alpine meadows, with snow remaining all year in some sheltered places. There is a profusion of wildflowers and bunchgrass with stands of conifers and poplars. As the altitude changes downriver the trees become taller and spruce tends to dominate. Below the canyon the river runs through the coastal rain belt, typified by cedar and dense undergrowth.

Wildlife is typical of most northern rivers with moose seen commonly along the water ways. Those taking the time to hike into the hills will find mountain goats, stone sheep, caribou and grizzly bear. River birds such as Canada geese, mergansers, harlequins and mallards keep the canoeist company, while along the shore and in the sky eagles, ravens, swallows, owls, shorebirds, terns, and gulls can be seen. Above the canyon Dollies, lake and rainbow trout, and grayling can be caught, and below the canyon is a spawning area for salmon.

The history and use of the upper Stikine is brief, for while the lower sections became river highways, the upper portion was blocked by the awesome unnavigable Grand Canyon of the Stikine. Only Indians, big game guides, some prospectors and a few adventurers have seen the upper reaches of the river. The lower portions became known and inhabited with

the discovery of gold near Glenora in 1860. After this came the soon-to-be aborted Collins Overland Telegraph Line, the Dease goldstrikes of 1874, the Klondike rush of 1897-98 and the freighting of World War II. Today the river is the centre of a vast region rich in resources. Timber, mineral claims and hydro-electric power sites await only the inevitable demand and consequent development. On the Stikine River alone there are seven areas reserved as potential dam sites. Canoeists wanting to see this river in its pristine, primitive glory should paddle it soon, and experience the river the Tlingits called "*the* river."

Books that give more information on the Stikine-Spatsizi country include Tommy Walker's *Spatsizi,* and R.M. Patterson's *Trail to the Interior.*

Where the Stikine begins, and where canoeists will leave their mechanical transportation, is a scenic lake surrounded by alpine meadows and snow-capped mountains. Tuaton Lake, about 10 km long, connects to Laslui Lake, 14 km long, by a 10 km stream with only minor riffles. The outlet from Laslui Lake differs in that only 1 mile below a portage must be made around a 1 km cut through bed-rock that makes an impassable rapid and boil 3 metres high. Carry along a ridge on the right 1.2 km.

From here there is 11 km of strenuous canoeing, to a point 3 km below Chapea Creek. At this point is another major rapid that must be portaged on the left, rejoining the river above some islands. Another 7 km of intermediate rapids, standing waves, swift water and large rounded rocks, extends to a pink granite canyon. The walls are up to 15 metres in height, and extend for about 1 km, causing swells, boils and standing waves which are usually navigated without problem. Be sure to scout this out. Below here a short distance is the junction of Metsantan Creek.

Near the junction of this creek and the Stikine was the site of the first settlement of the Caribou Hide Indians. Originally from the Bear Lake region they travelled here in search of a place far away from village fighting and drinking. They settled here prior to WWI, later moving up the creek to Metsantan Lake and finally to the Iskut Valley.

For the next 32 km the paddling is fast and easy with only minor riffles until the Chukachida River is reached. This is 76 km from Tuaton Lake. From this junction to the Stewart-Cassiar Highway is 190 km, with an average drop of 2.3 metres per km. Below the river is slow for 10 km but soon the velocity increases and large standing waves appear.

At the junction of the Spatsizi and Stikine impressive views are seen of the Spatsizi highlands. Three km downstream there is an outfitters' camp with a radio-phone. Float planes can land on the river here.

The river widens now, becoming susceptible to winds which often blow upstream, impeding the course of canoes. About 16 km downstream from the camp is Jewel Canyon, about 2 km in length and 100 metres wide, bordered by 4 metre gravel banks. Scout this section. Canoes can usually get along the left shore, then ferry over to the right to avoid rough water. This can be portaged on either side.

From here to the Pitman River, which flows in from the north, the current stays strong with minor riffles. 4 km downstream is Schreiber Canyon where a rock bluff on the right creates standing waves. It may be passed on the left. Now it is easy paddling to Beggerlay Creek with the river wide and braided in some places.

At Beggerlay Creek a canyon begins that necessitates a carry along the left bank, to avoid carrying over Beggerlay. Goat Canyon has fierce rapids and powerful surges. Scout the portage as it may be difficult going. It is about 1 km in length.

Just 1.5 km below Goat Canyon the Klappen River flows in from the south, with the bridge of the B.C. Railway nearby. Another canyon is 3 km downstream, and can be canoed on the left. 18 km later the bridge of the Stewart-Cassiar Highway is reached. Take-out here. Downstream is the Grand Canyon of the Stikine. Arrangements for pick-up must be made ahead of time as there are no services offered here. The other side of this 95 km canyon is Telegraph Creek, 170 km away.

The Grand Canyon has never been navigated. In 95 km it drops an average of 10 metres per km, with canyon walls 300 to 400 metres high and narrows where the usual width of 60 metres squeezes into 15 metres. There are chutes, boiling whitewater and falls violent enough to keep sections ice-free all winter.

At Telegraph Creek the river has taken on a different quality, wider, deeper and straighter with a velocity of about 10 km per hour. There are many riffles and rapids in the next section according to maps but most of these rapids came by their names and designation during the days of stern-wheelers and usually are easily canoed, though it is a good idea to still check them out. Like all large rivers the volume and speed of the water creates boils, whirlpools and eddies which can easily flip a boat. Watch for one particularly bad section just below Yehiniko Creek. This type of river extends downriver from Telegraph Creek for 40 km.

Below Chutine River the Channel is braided with lots of islands and gravel bars and a slow current. Now the main hazards are deadheads and log jams. At Little Canyon the river narrows to 50 metres for 0.5 km with 35 metre cliffs. Then the river begins to meander, until Boundary House site is reached, 5 km upstream from the Alaska border. This is now abandoned and egress is either to fly-out, by previous arrangement, or continue paddling across the border to Alaska. This will necessitate another 65 km paddle, part of it through fairly open ocean waters to Wrangel, south of the Stikine mouth. From Wrangell it is possible to fly back, take an infrequent, irregular river boat back to Telegraph Creek, or a ferry south to Prince Rupert. Additional maps and route information should be sought if you plan on continuing on to Wrangell.

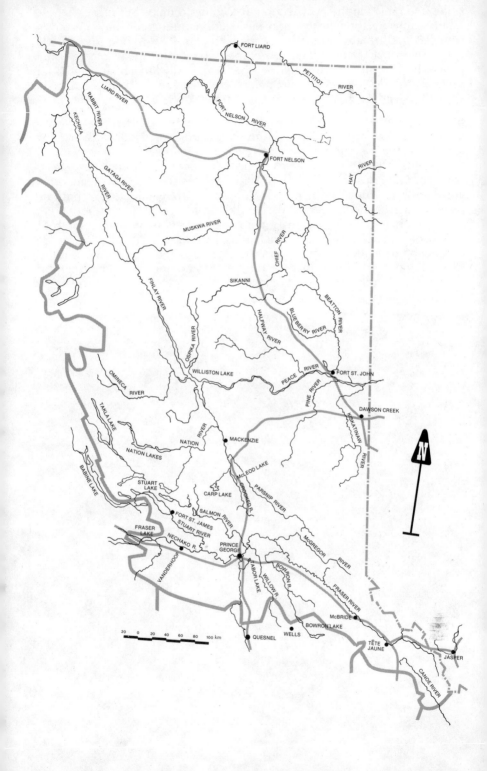

FORT LIARD

PETTITOT RIVER

LIARD RIVER

RABBIT RIVER

KECHIKA

FORT NELSON RIVER

GATAGA RIVER

RIVER

FORT NELSON

HAY RIVER

MUSKWA RIVER

CHIEF RIVER

FINLAY RIVER

SIKANNI

BEATON RIVER

OSPIKA RIVER

HALFWAY RIVER

BLUEBERRY RIVER

OMINECA RIVER

WILLISTON LAKE

PEACE RIVER

FORT ST. JOHN

TAKLA LAKE

PINE RIVER

DAWSON CREEK

RIVER

KISKATINAW RIVER

NATION LAKES

NATION

MACKENZIE

BABINE LAKE

STUART LAKE

McLEOD LAKE

CARP LAKE

CROOKED R.

PARSNIP RIVER

FORT ST. JAMES

SALMON RIVER

STUART RIVER

FRASER LAKE

NECHAKO R.

PRINCE GEORGE

McGREGOR RIVER

VANDERHOOF

TABOR LAKE

WILLOW R.

BOWRON R.

FRASER RIVER

McBRIDE

BOWRON LAKE

TÊTE JAUNE

QUESNEL

WELLS

JASPER

CANOE RIVER

20 0 20 40 60 80 100 km

N

134

OMINECA-PEACE REGION

ROUTE - BOWRON RIVER *Natural River*
GRADE - *3*
LENGTH - *174 km, 2 to 6 portages*
WIDTH - *15 to 30 metres*
VERTICAL DROP - *287 metres*
TIME TO ALLOW - *3 to 5 days*
NEAREST EMERGENCY COMMUNICATION - *Wells 27 km; Highway 16 near terminus; McGregor, across Fraser; Purden Lake Provincial Park or Prince George*
CAMPING - ACCOMMODATION - *Bowron Lake Provincial Park near put-in; unorganized along route; Purden Lake Provincial Park near take-out*
MAPS - *N.T.S 1:250,000 93H McBride; 93G Prince George; 93J McLeod Lake; 93I Monkman Pass*
HAZARDS - *Rapids, log jams, remote*

DIRECTIONS

From Quesnel on Highway 97 drive to Bowron Lake Provincial Park. Put-in at lake, or follow the road along the river for several miles to avoid the first few log jams. Take-out at Highway 16 or if expert continue to the Fraser at Hansard.

DESCRIPTION

Almost since the first canoeist ventured down the wild Bowron it has been proposed as an example of the type of river that should be preserved and protected by "wild river" legislation. So far it has not, but perhaps in the future it will be afforded some recreational status.

This is not a historical river, though certainly the general country it passes through is rich in history. Early travellers avoided it because of the difficult navigation. During the gold rush this was known as the Bear River and was later renamed to honor John Bowron, an Overlander who settled in Barkerville and became one of the Cariboo's leading citizens.

On its course from the Bowron Lake chain to the Fraser River the Bowron skirts along the west side of the Cariboo Mountains, crossing the Fraser Plateau. The drainage basin lies in the Columbia Forest region, or what is part of the Sub-Alpine Forest biotic zone. Spruce dominates the vegetation and precipitation is higher than in most of the Interior Plateau. More rain means more flies and mosquitoes so be prepared. Along the river alder and willow grow on the banks and sandbars and a few cottonwoods and birch are seen.

Wildlife seen includes moose, black and grizzly bear, mule deer, perhaps some caribou, eagles and those ducks and geese that inhabit the province's waterways. The mouths of the streams offer good angling for rainbow and Dolly Varden trout and in August salmon spawn in the headwaters.

This is not a river for novices. Log jams and rapids make it tricky and sometimes dangerous. Low water means it will be difficult to get through the rock gardens and highwater will make the canyons difficult. It is best canoed with a guide.

In the first 16 km of the river there are at least 6 log jams. These completely block the river and while some may be easily passed at least three require a portage. Just upstream of Eighteen Mile Creek a stretch of rough water begins, but it can be easily run.

Thirty-eight km below Bowron Lake a 13 km rapid begins. The first section is boulder-strewn and will require good maneuvering to avoid the rocks. At 45 km a canyon begins which runs to 63 km. The canyon is grade 3+ and must be scouted before an attempt to run it is made. The right side will usually be the best. Be careful of whirlpools, eddies and rocks on the left side. There is no portage around this canyon. Be prepared to scout the next section. At 64 km Haggen Creek flows in on the right. An old bridge here has caused a log jam around the pilings but check the left for a passage. A road on the east side here connects with Highway 16, 60 km north.

Haggen Creek is clear and cold, draining lakes in the Cariboo Mountains. Its stream adds volume to the Bowron and the river picks up speed. Two small rapids are quickly passed and then below Spruce Creek another. Three km downstream from this last rapid there is a long log jam. Check on the left for a passage, but this could be blocked off. From here the river passes through a large burn. High gravel banks become more frequent. At 101 km there is an abandoned coal mine on the left bank. Canoeists not wanting to run the next difficult section could take-out on the right bank where there is road access.

One km below Taspai Creek, which enters on the left, the first of three long rapids begins. These rapids are rated grade three and require a great deal of skill to navigate. From the third rapid the Highway 16 bridge may be seen. If you are to end your trip here take-out on the left bank just below the bridge.

The section of river below the bridge is more difficult than the upper river and is suitable for experts only. Open canoes will ship water. Five named canyons must be run. Bear, Basket, Portage, Boat and Box Canyon. There is 23 km of rapids with 16 individual drops or ledges. At least two portages will be necessary.

Of the sixteen sections the first 2 begin just below the bridge in Bear Canyon. The left side is best. The third is a short canyon with high black walls and a left turn and again left is best. The fourth is navigable by a variety of routes and below this there is 3 km of fast smooth water. The fifth and sixth are short and close together and a portage may be necessary. Open canoes will ship water. The right is probably best here. At the seventh rough section the river is split by an island and the right will be best.

The next three sections of the sixteen contain chutes and either side may be run. One km below is a rapid that cannot be run. Portage 60 metres along the left shore. Scout the next rapid where the river widens. Another portage may be necessary unless you are really good. Now there is a 3 km section of fast but smooth water leading to the last 4 rough sections.

A boulder field is first and here you can try the right, then there is a small ledge where a chute on the extreme right allows passage. The third must be portaged 30 metres on the right. Below this is a short canyon with high wall and turbulent water. One half a km below this canyon is the last rapid of this section. Run it on the left to the right of a large rock.

Now Cottonwood Island is passed and 0.5 km downstream of the island Box Canyon is run, with powerful eddies and boils. From here to the Fraser is 48 km. The river for the most part now meanders and slows considerably. A logging road crosses below Boy Canyon. Five km downstream is a dangerous log jam. Start watching for it. The only route, unless the river has changed things, is through a 1 metre passage on the extreme left. Be particularly careful in this area. Log jams do not give second chances. The river is strong and can quickly and easily pull a canoe under. Do not try to run on the right side as there is an unseen 1 metre ledge. Check this log jam out carefully before attempting to go through.

Below this log jam the river meanders until the Fraser is reached. Three km downstream on the Fraser the C.N.R. bridge crosses from McGregor, now a ghost town, to Hansard. Vehicular traffic now uses this bridge as well as the railway so it is a good place to pull out. The road on the left bank leads to Giscome and Prince George.

ROUTE - SALMON RIVER *Recreational River*
GRADE - *1 to 2*
LENGTH - *170 km, 9 to 12 portages*
WIDTH - *10 to 25 metres*
VERTICAL DROP - *152 metres; 1 metre per km*

TIME TO ALLOW - *1 week*
NEAREST EMERGENCY COMMUNICATION - *Salmon Valley terminus or Prince George, 27 km south*
CAMPING - ACCOMMODATION - *Unorganized*
MAPS - *N.T.S. 1:250,000 McLeod Lake 93J*
HAZARDS - *Log jams, remote*

DIRECTIONS

Fly-in to Great Beaver Lake from Prince George or take the Salmon River road west to a point a few miles below Great Beaver Lake at a river bank hunting camp. Lower access from this same road is possible at the confluence of the Salmon and Muskeg Rivers. Egress at the Salmon Valley Bridge on the Hart Highway, or continue south on Fraser to Prince George.

DESCRIPTION

This report covers the lower two-thirds of the Salmon. A recent new forestry road from McLeod Lake to Carp Lake and Fort St. James crosses the Salmon near its headwaters in Salmon Lake, in fact a side road leads right to the lake. Canoeists wanting to travel the whole river might want to check out the upper section for the feasibility of beginning further upstream. It is likely too shallow.

The Salmon River flows through the Nechako Plateau region, first in a southerly and then an easterly direction. The northern section is in an area of glacial deposition, while the lower is thought to have been part of a large glacial lake. It is within the Montane Forest Region, or the Subalpine Forest biotic zone. Lodgepole pine, spruce and Douglas fir are the common trees, with aspen and willow in the poorly drained areas. The river banks often support large stands of cottonwood and poplar.

Wildlife along the river includes a wide variety of fur bearers, moose, mule deer, black bear and grizzly bear. Many Canada geese can be seen as well as mergansers, eagles and osprey. Kokanee and lake trout can be caught in Great Beaver Lake and rainbow and Dollies in the river.

From Great Beaver Lake, Great Beaver Creek must be followed to the Salmon River. It leaves the lake about half way down the east side of the lake in a large bay. The creek is about 5 metres wide with a kilometre of meanders and then a few riffles. At the confluence with the Salmon the river is about 10 metres wide, and just 2.5 km downstream the first of the Salmon's many log jams is encountered. In the course of the journey approximately 15 will have to be portaged. In the next 14 km there are 5 log jams. Be cautious on corners.

At kilometre 15 the Boundary River flows in from the north. At 5, 10 and 18 kilometres below this point watch for log jams. As the Salmon nears the confluence with the Muskeg the velocity increases. Just upstream of the junction a bridge crosses to the north side of the river. This can be an alternate put-in point, or if need be a terminus.

Below the Muskeg River 10 km is another major log jam, and, 13 km downstream another. All of these log jams can be portaged along the banks. Scouting will indicate the best carry. Three kilometres below Crocker Creek, near where the river begins a northward course or a few kilometres, both channels of the river are completely blocked. Then another small jam and the river flows unobstructed for 18 kilometres. Caution must still be exercised as any of these jams could be washed out and new ones may have been formed since the last river passage. Do not rely on others information too heavily, but scout ahead.

Watch for a logging road crossing the river. A log jam is 6.5 km downstream. The last of these river blockages is another 10 km below. There is an old logging road along the left shore that can be used. This is actually two jams with a total carry of about 500 metres. Beyond the jam the river increases in velocity and some small, shallow rapids occur, all of which can be run if the water is high enough. There are some sharp turns that must be watched though. Lining or portages may be necessary depending on water levels and paddling experience. Watch for the Hart Highway bridge for the trips terminus. Access is easy for vehicles at this point. An alternate terminus is to canoe south about 25 kilometres and take-out in Prince George.

ROUTE - CROOKED RIVER *Recreational River*

GRADE - *1 +*

LENGTH - *95 km*

WIDTH - *10 to 20 metres*

VERTICAL DROP - *30 metres, 3.3 decimetres per km*

TIME TO ALLOW - *2 to 4 days*

NEAREST EMERGENCY COMMUNICATION - *Summit Lake, Bear Lake Park, McLeod Lake*

CAMPING - ACCOMMODATION - *Bear Lake Park; Whiskers Point on McLeod Lake or organized sites along the river*

MAPS - *N.T.S 1:250,000 93J McLeod Lake*

HAZARDS - *Some power boats, sweepers*

DIRECTIONS

Drive north from Prince George 48 km to Summit Lake. Put-in at north end of lake where a side road leads to a bridge. Take-out is possible at many places but end of trip is at McLeod Lake settlement.

DESCRIPTION

Simon Fraser first established a post on this route, at McLeod Lake in 1805. He called it Trout Lake and Trout Lake Post but both were later named McLeod. This was the first permanent settlement west of the Rockies in what is now British Columbua. Fraser visited the Pack River and McLeod Lake in 1806 when he embarked on his initial exploration of the great river that was to bear his name.

Today it is possible to paddle the complete route from Summit Lake to McLeod, and then on through Tudyah Lake and down the Pack river if a slightly longer trip is wanted. Until the 1950's when the Hart Highway was built this route, connecting the Parsnip, Finlay and Peace Rivers, was the only route to the north.

Along the river and lakes wildlife of many kinds may be seen, including moose, black and grizzly bears, wolves, beaver, mink and smaller furbearers. Waterfowl and songbirds are abundant while the waters provide good fishing for rainbow trout, Dolly Varden and arctic grayling.

This area is now known as the Crooked River Recreational Zone, undertaken by the Crooked River Forest Association and the B.C. Forest Service. Bear Lake Park is of course looked after by the Provincial Parks branch.

Along the first part of the river from Summit Lake to Bear Lake Park some portages may be necessary, because of numerous beaver dams. Watch for sweepers. From a point halfway along this first section to Davie Lake the river alternates between wide, slow, shallow water and fast, shallow water. Davie Lake is the first point where power boats can put in. Downstream of Davie the water picks up a little speed and then runs into Redrocky Lake, which pretty well extends to Kerry Lake.

From Kerry Lake to McLeod the river is wide with slow to moderate current, then passes under a low bridge to McLeod Lake. Whiskers Point Provincial campground is located on the right side of the lake about half way down. It has a sand beach and makes a very pleasant stop.

The take-out can be at McLeod Lake, a settlement on the right bank, where a road runs down to the north end of the lake. The trip can be continued on for approximately 30 km through Tudyah lake and down the Pack River to the Parsnip River, now highwater of the Williston Reservoir. This stream is faster with rapids to grade 2, possibly grade 3 in some water conditions. Formerly this was just the beginning of a fine canoe journey down the Parsnip to Finlay Forks and then down the Peace River to Rocky Mountain Portage. All of it now lies under the water of the W.A.C. Bennett Dam and Williston Reservoir.

ROUTE - CARP LAKE - CARP LAKE PARK

GRADE - *Lake and 1*

LENGTH - *Carp Lake 9.5 x 11 km; McLeod River and War Lake 10.5 km*

WIDTH - *10 metres to 9.5 km*

VERTICAL DROP - *Negligible*

TIME TO ALLOW - *1 day to 1 week*

NEAREST EMERGENCY COMMUNICATION - *McLeod Lake 26 km northwest*

CAMPING - ACCOMMODATION - *B.C.F.S. campground at northwest end, or unorganized*

MAPS - *N.T.S. 1:250,000 93J McLeod Lake*

HAZARDS - *Falls below War Lake, power boats*

DIRECTIONS

Follow Hart Highway north of Prince George 140 km. Turn left onto gravel road that leads to Carp Lake and ultimately Fort St. James. Travel west and south 26 km. Put-in at B.C.F.S. boat launch.

DESCRIPTION

Carp Lake Provincial Park is one of the province's newest, established in 1973. The park is comprised of Carp Lake and a surrounding area, an 8 km section of the McLeod River, and 2.5 km long War Lake, all of which offer good canoeing. Carp Lake might be described as a bulbous H shape, with about 100 km of shoreline and over 20 islands of various sizes. There are extensive sand and gravel beaches, particularly along the north shore, and this, with good fishing, makes it an extremely popular lake of the Prince George Region.

Historically the lake was an important trail link between Fort McLeod and Fort St. James, and provided a life sustaining fishery for both the natives and the fur traders. Father Morice refers to War Lake as Long Lake and the Mcleod River he calls Long River.

The park lies on the Nechako Plateau at an elevation of 823 metres, an area shaped by the ice that covered it a million years ago. Carp Lake is a deep gouge in the glacial till plain that contains thousands of grooves and ridges. The summer here is short and cool, with the least precipitation falling in spring.

Vegetation includes lodgepole pine and aspen groves with some spruce. Thimbleberry and salmon berry provide good cover. Wildlife in the area likely to be seen by the canoeist will be moose, black bear, mule deer, wolves, beaver and many smaller mammals.

Being a popular lake conoeist will not be the only ones using the water, so care should be taken to avoid power boats. Some water skiiers may use the lake but it is hoped that a restricted area will be set aside. Just downstream of the outlet of War Lake are War Falls. Be sure to keep away from the outlet. The two cascades that form the falls are 5 metres and 12 metres in height, separated by 100 metres of white water.

ROUTE - NECHAKO RIVER - CHESLATTA FALLS TO STUART RIVER
Recreational River

GRADE - *2*

LENGTH - *65 km to Fort Fraser; 50 km Fort Fraser to Vanderhoof; 25 km Vanderhoof to Stuart River*

WIDTH - *20 to 40 metres*

VERTICAL DROP - *92 metres; 1.4 metres per km to Fort Fraser. Approximately 30 metres to Stuart River confluence*

TIME TO ALLOW - *2 to 5 days*

NEAREST EMERGENCY COMMUNICATION - *Fort Fraser and Vanderhoof*

CAMPING - ACCOMMODATION - *B.C.F.S. campsite or unorganized along route. Beaumont Provincial Park at Fort Fraser terminus*

MAPS - *N.T.S. 1:250,000 93F Nechako River; 93K Fort Fraser; 93G Prince George*

HAZARDS - *Some rapids*

DIRECTIONS

From Highway 16 at Vanderhoof take the Kenny Dam Road south approximately 96 km to one of two launch points. Terminate at Fort Fraser, Vanderhoof or Prince George.

DESCRIPTION

This description of the Nechako extends to its confluence with the Stuart River. For the continuation to Prince George see the Stuart - Nechako description.

This is the "Incha-khoh", the "Big River" of the Carrier Indians. It is the river that led Simon Fraser from the Fraser River to the Stuart River and later Fraser Lake. For canoeists today it is a relatively easy paddle through interesting historic country.

The upper part of the Nechako River now lies beneath the flood waters of Knewstubb Lake, part of the Kemano-Kitimat project that flooded so much of Tweedsmuir Park. The Kenny Dam blocks the lake and river, leaving a dry canyon downstream until Cheslatta Falls spills into the riverbed. This is the highest launching point, though access is difficult.

After crossing Kenny Dam turn right onto a dirt road that leads 8 kilometres to a small B.C.F.S. campsite and some spectacular cascades on what is now called the Nechako River, as it flows from Murray Lake. Park here. The portage trail heads off from the end of road, across a dirt barrier dam and along a ridge to the canyon. From here it drops down to the old bed of the river. It is about a half hours walk, without a canoe. Here the canoe can be launched right at the base of 18 metre high Cheslatta Falls. Take some time to explore the old river bed.

For the first 15 km of river there are three rapids. Beyond that the river is fairly straight forward. The first rapids may be avoided by launching at a second, easier downriver site. About 16 kilometers south of the dam, 80 km from Vanderhoof, there is a B.C.F.S. campground with toilets, tables and a launching ramp for river boats. This is a good point to launch canoes.

Fishing is good along the river for rainbow and Dolly Varden. Watch for moose, beaver, wolves, black bear, deer, coyotes, and domestic cattle. A short distance downstream from the second launch point is River Ranch, established by Rich Hobson, author of the books, *Grass Beyond the Mountains, Nothing Too Good for a Cowboy,* and *Rancher Takes a Wife,* classics in the story of B.C.

As the river flows north it gradually leaves the timbered forest and enters a small piece of Cariboo Parklands, a biotic zone that is centered around Vanderhoof. The first take-out point is the Highway 16 bridge, a warning of which is given by the railway bridge across the river.

Beaumont Provincial Park and campground is on the left, down river. Below this point the Nautley River flows in from Fraser Lake, a river only a kilometre long, bordered by an Indian reserve protecting fishing rights. During its course to Vanderhoof the Nechako flows through agricultural land, past large farms and ranches. Not quite half way to Vanderhoof is a rapid that should be checked out. It occurs soon after the river begins to flow south for a short distance.

Near Vanderhoof a migratory bird sanctuary is passed. During the northern migration of Canada geese in April the river flats are the feeding and resting place for thousands of the large waterfowl. In the fall smaller numbers stop here. Vanderhoof offers supplies, accommodation and communications for paddlers.

Downstream again the river is wide and deep with one set of rapids to scout below Hulatt station, on the right bank. Then it is clear paddling again to Finmore station and crossing, another possible pull-out, and on the Stuart River confluence.

ROUTE - STUART - NECHAKO RIVERS *Recreational River*

GRADE - *1, rapids to 3*

LENGTH - *195 km*

WIDTH - *40 to 100 metres*

VERTICAL DROP - *110 metres; 5.6 decimetres per km*

TIME TO ALLOW - *3 to 6 days*

NEAREST EMERGENCY COMMUNICATION - *Fort St. James, Isle Pierre Ferry, Prince George*

CAMPING - ACCOMMODATION - *Unorganized along route. Commercial campground at Stuart Canyon and in Prince George. Accommodation in Fort St. James and Prince George*

MAPS - *N.T.S. 1:250,000 93G Prince George; 93J McLeod Lake; 93K Fort Fraser*

HAZARDS - *Rapids*

DIRECTIONS

From Vanderhoof on Highway 16 drive north on 27 to Fort St. James, 66 km. Put-in on lakeshore at any convenient point. Prince George is the route's terminus.

DESCRIPTION

Modern voyageurs with a sense and appreciation of history can travel this route and find it much the same as Simon Fraser did in July of 1806 when he travelled from Fort MacLeod to Stuart Lake, then known as Carrier Lake. Fraser established a post here, later named Fort St. James, that became the capital and major centre of New Caledonia. The lake and river he named after John Stuart, a clerk and Fraser's second in command during his three years exploring New Caledonia. At present the fort is being restored by the Federal Government as a National Historic Park and will represent the period of the mid 1890's. The reconstruction would make a fitting starting point for a canoe journey.

The Stuart and Nechako Rivers lie on the rolling Nechako Plateau and flow through a flat bottomed basin that was once a glacial lake. The rivers are in the Montane Forest Region, the Subalpine forest biotic zone where the dominent trees consist of spruce and lodgepole pine. Burned over areas along the banks are covered in aspen growth with willows and alder along the shore. These second growth areas provide excellent browse for both moose and mule deer, often seen on the river. Wildlife is the usual for this region, including black bear, grizzly, wolves, coyotes, and furbearers such as beaver and otter. Harlequins, mergansers and Canada geese often spring up in front of a canoe while ospreys and eagles soar overhead. Kingfishers and black terns frequent the river and grouse use the forest along the shore.

Fishing is good for rainbow trout and Dolly Varden. Salmon migrate in late July and August and lake trout and kokanee are found in the lakes. There are also some coarse fish such as suckers and whitefish.

From the launch point at the southeast end of the lake paddle south past the Indian Reserve into the Stuart River, through a narrow stretch with fast water and then under the highway bridge. This kilometre of river leads past pilings, docks and a mill to the Stuart River Canyon. The grade in the canyon will vary from 2 to 4 depending on water levels. the right channel is usually best, or lining along the right shore. A road reaches the lower end of the canyon from the last mill on the right so it would be possible to portage this section or put-in lower down.

The next 68 km of river is clear paddling on grade 1 water. Abandoned farms and meadows provide good camping spots on this section. The river is slow enough to paddle upstream. At the end of this 68 km section a road from Vanderhoof reaches the river, marked by a burnt bridge. To avoid the downriver rapids return to Vanderhoof by this road.

After Chinohchey Creek flows in from the left the river turns sharply south and the speed increases. From here to Saxton Creek, about 15 km, there are 4 rapids on 4 river bends. The fast and rough water is best taken on the inside of the curve, avoiding the standing waves on the outside.

South of Saxton the velocity increases again and 4 more rapids must be run. The first two are similar to the last set of 4 and can be run in a similar fashion. The third and fourth are the Chinlac Rapids, beginning 7 km from the Nechako confluence. These are long and difficult, considered by some to be impassable without a guide. The first section can be run on either side to avoid standing waves in centre channel but a great amount of man-ouvering may be necessary to avoid boulders. The last section is a series of ledges. The right side is best but at low water it could be very difficult. Scout both of these before running. It is possible to line canoes through this section.

On an early map of this country drawn by Father Morice this last section of river from Saxton Creek south is by-passed by a trail. It is possible that early travellers portaged the rapids or had canoes at both ends. On the right bank of the Stuart, just above the junction with the Nechako there was once an Indian village called Chinlac. The people were Carriers, related to those of the Stuart Lake area. In 1745 a large war party of Chilcotins raided the village while some of the men were away, killing almost the entire village. Although revenged three years later the village was never rebuilt. The clearing nearby now provides a camping spot for canoeists.

As the two rivers join the speed slows and the river widens to 25 to 40 metres. Until 5 km above Isle de Pierre Rapids the water is smooth. Then a rapid occurs with 4 distinct ledges, best run on the right side. One mile below the Isle Pierre Ferry are the Isle de Pierre Rapids, consisting of 3 sections. The first 2 are 100 metres apart and here the river is divided by an island. The left channel is the best route. The third section is 1 km below the first two and begins with a log pile. Again the left channel is the best. the Whitemud Rapids are next, marked by Bednesti station on the right. These rapids can be portaged on the right bank, along the railway tracks. Sections must be run, the first along the left bank and then crossing between the two sets to run the second series through a chute on the right. The next 5 km are marked by fast water and boulders, then the river slows into large meander bends before a straight section leading to Prince George. An appropriate terminus for this trip would be to turn down the Fraser a kilometer and take out at the reconstructed Fort George Park.

ROUTE - NATION LAKE CHAIN *Scenic Shoreline*

GRADE - *1 & 2*

LENGTH - *140 km one way*

WIDTH - *Varying*

VERTICAL DROP - *Minimal*

TIME TO ALLOW - *Approximately one week*

NEAREST EMERGENCY COMMUNICATION - *Fort St. James*

CAMPING - ACCOMMODATION - *Wilderness. Some campsites and limited accommodation at launching point*

MAPS - *N.T.S. 1:250,000 93N Manson River*

HAZARDS - *Remote, few log jams*

DIRECTIONS

Leave the Yellowhead, Highway 16, at Vanderhoof and go north past Fort St. James 120 km. Watch for signs to the left, west to Chuchi Lake.

DESCRIPTION

This route is remote wilderness. Paddlers should be experienced in wilderness travel and know rescue and repair procedures. The trip starts in Chuchi lake, 28 km, enters the river for 5 then Tchentlo Lake for 32, the river for 11, Indata lake for 16, the river 16, and finally Tsayta Lake for 30 km. The rivers are shallow with some deadfall and grade 2 rapids, though it is an easy paddle. It is suggested as an ideal trip on which to take children.

The lakes have sheltered coves with sandy beaches suitable for camping. Moose, bear and wolves may be seen. Vegetation is similar to southern B.C. with spruce, pine, willows, alder and poplar. Good fishing.

An alternative to paddling the return length of 280 km is to contact Mr. A. Fowlie, Box 1106, Prince George B.C. V2L 4V2. He has a jet boat that is capable of carrying four people, their gear and two canoes, and he will run you up to the far end of the lakes so you can paddle back. He also has some camping sites and limited accommodation at the launching site on Chuchi Lake. While you are on the trip he will also look after your vehicles. Contact him for the cost.

A second means of access is to fly-in from Fort St. James to Tsayta Lake, then paddling the whole route downstream to Chuchi Lake and either flying or hitchhiking out. There is little traffic on the road however.

ROUTE - PEACE RIVER *Recreational River*
GRADE - *1*
LENGTH - *100 km*
WIDTH - *100 metres to 1 km*
VERTICAL DROP - *Minimal*
TIME TO ALLOW - *3 days*
NEAREST EMERGENCY COMMUNICATION - *Hudson Hope, Taylor*
CAMPING - ACCOMMODATION - *Unorganized*
MAPS - *N.T.S. 1:250,000 94A Charlie Lake*
HAZARDS - *Sudden flooding from Bennett dam*

DIRECTIONS

Take Highway 97 to Chetwynd then 29 north to Hudson Hope. Put-in here and take-out at Taylor or Peace Island Park across the river from Taylor, on the Alaska Highway.

DESCRIPTION

Once the only navigable river to cross the Rockies the Peace is a mere shadow of its former character due to the W.A.C. Bennett Dam at Mountain Portage. This river was the first highway to New Caledonia, now British Columbia. It was the route taken by Mackenzie on his trip to the Pacific Ocean and Simon Fraser when he explored the Fraser River system. And for almost a century it was the main route from the interior of the province to the north country. The flood waters of the reservoir covered the Parsnip, Findlay and Peace Rivers, three of the finest canoe routes in the province.

This lower portion of the Peace is nevertheless an interesting paddle for canoeists. It is easily paddled anytime between May and October, though paddlers should take care to camp well above the water line as the dam can cause sudden flooding. Campsites are easily found. Old forts, trading posts, trappers cabins and homesteads are part of the river scenery. Four fort sites are passed: The original Fort St. John at the mouth of the Beaton river, 1806-23; another, opposite Old Fort, in operation 1857-87; a site below modern Fort St. John and Rocky Mountain Portage House at the mouth of Morice Creek, opposite Hudson Hope.

Wildlife likely to be seen includes, deer, moose, elk, black bear, beaver and perhaps even lynx. Birds frequently seen are ducks, geese, bald eagles, kingfishers, kingbirds and woodpeckers.

This is a popular river trip and some peak weekends will see up to 20 to 30 canoes per day pass any given point. Take-out can be at Peace Island Park near Taylor. Canoeists wanting to go further can continue east to the Alberta border, 45 km or Vermillion Alberta, 640 km.

ROUTE - PINE RIVER - EAST PINE TO TAYLOR *Natural River*
GRADE - *2*
LENGTH - *85 km*
WIDTH - *Varies*
VERTICAL DROP - *Approximately 50 metres*
TIME TO ALLOW - *2 to 3 days*
NEAREST EMERGENCY COMMUNICATION - *Chetwynd and Taylor*
CAMPING - ACCOMMODATION - *Moberly Lake Park 20 km north of Chetwynd; unorganized along route*
MAPS - *N.T.S. 1:250,000 93P Dawson Creek; 94A Charlie Lake*
HAZARDS - *Difficult canoeing in flood; some standing waves on bends*

DIRECTIONS

Put-in at East Pine bridge, 56 km west of Dawson Creek, 33 km east of Chetwynd on Hart Highway. Paddle downstream to Taylor on Peace River.

DESCRIPTION

Although by some accounts the Pine River is navigable from Chetwynd this description begins at East Pine bridge. Here the Murray River flows in from the south, from the area of Monkman Pass. River speed is 6 to 8 km per hour, faster during flood. The river banks are high, as much as a couple of hundred metres, and coal seams can often be seen where the river has cut through. Oil sometimes seeps from the banks as well.

Sandy beaches on island or river shores offer good camping spots, with a chance of seeing deer, beaver, black bear, weasel, coyotes or wolves along the water. River birds are seen, including kingfishers and sandpipers.

Take-out at the Taylor bridge over the Peace, or cross the river to Taylor townsite, or Peace Island Park, on the right bank of the Pine at the confluence with the Peace.

ROUTE - FORT NELSON RIVER - FORT NELSON TO FORT LIARD
GRADE - *1 +*
LENGTH - *284 km*
WIDTH - *100 metres to 1 km*
VERTICAL DROP - *64 metres*
TIME TO ALLOW - *4 to 6 days*
NEAREST EMERGENCY COMMUNICATION - *Fort Nelson and Fort Liard*
CAMPING - ACCOMMODATION - *Unorganized. Good campsites on gravel bars*
MAPS - *N.T.S 1:250,000 94J Fort Nelson; 94O Maxhamish Lake; 94N Toad River; 95B Fort Liard*
HAZARDS - *Remote, some sweepers*

DIRECTIONS

Drive north on the Alaska Highway to Fort Nelson, 483 km north of Dawson Creek B.C. Put-in on Muskwa River, south of town. At Fort Liard it will be necessary to fly-out, by pre-arrangement. Fort Simpson is 315 km downstream from Fort Liard.

DESCRIPTION

Although not an exciting river in terms of whitewater rapids or mountain scenery the Fort Nelson River has an appeal to the wilderness canoeist. Travel is easy and unhurried, with no fear of coming upon unexpected rapids. There is time to leisurely float, contemplate the surroundings and one's being there and paddle when the spirit moves. Here we can easily imagine the passing of the traders canoes heading upstream to old Fort Nelson, and on the river banks there are still the cabins, camps and boats

of native trappers and hunters. Several old settlements and trading posts are passed, the highlight of which is a day or two at Fort Liard, soon to see a road pushed through from Fort Simpson. Soon this part of the north will change and those who enjoy the present isolation should head there soon.

The river trip actually begins on the Muskwa River, just a few kilometres upstream of its confluence with the Fort Nelson. Where the Alaska Highway crosses the Muskwa there is access to the riverbank. Put-in here and head downstream. Do not leave your camp or canoes unattended overnight. Sleep near the boats.

These are muddy rivers and it would be advisable to carry fresh drinking water, refilling at many of the small streams which flow in. The banks of both rivers are lined with sweepers and broken trees tumbling into the ever changing flow. Just downstream of the confluence old Fort Nelson can be seen on the right bank. Now an Indian village this was the site of the original trading post that was named for Lord Nelson, the British admiral. Present day Fort Nelson began when the Alaska Highway was pushed through during World War II.

Kingfishers, gulls, sandpipers and various ducks are seen along this section of river downstream to Snake River. Snake River flows in from the southeast, giving its name to a small Indian village consisting of five cabins and a smoke house. They appear to only be used for winter trapping or hunting.

For the 100 km below Snake River the Fort Nelson meanders from side to side in a valley uniformly 2 km wide, bordered by banks 100 metres high.

The country beyond the valley walls is muskeg, miles and miles of swamp dotted with a myriad of lakes and criss-crossed with streams and rivers. Each river bend has a gravel bar, many covered in willows but others are high and dry and quite comfortable for a camp.

As the meander bends begin to straighten the valley banks begin to rise higher, though this is not always evident from the viewpoint of a canoe. The Fort Nelson straits are entered as the river begins a final 25 km run to the confluence with the Liard. On the right bank high yellow sandstone cliffs break the river bank monotony, a feature that early voyageurs called the "roche que trempe a l'eau". A cabin is passed just after the steepest portion.

A final S bend and then on the right can be seen the buildings that mark the site of Nelson Forks, usually used as a cache. Black bear and grizzly have been seen in this area. This remote region has already been planned as a settlement area, a railhead for the B.C. Railway and the site of a huge pulp operation. Power would come from dams on the Liard, downstream and/or upstream. Upstream, beyond where the Beaver River flows in, there is a flooding reserve to the "1500 foot contour", and downstream to the "1000 foot contour". It is more than a little difficult to imagine while camped at this spot. A large gravel bar just upstream from the confluence with the Liard provides a good campsite. There are too many mosquitoes at Nelson Forks for comfort.

As the Fort Nelson River flows into the Liard, the River of Cottonwoods, the water doubles in width, an imposing width for canoeists. Crossing the river is like crossing a small lake. A straighter course will be possible by staying near the middle of the river but it is much more interesting along the shore. Moose and caribou are sometimes seen in this area. Twenty km downstream from the confluence, La Joli Butte is seen on the right bank, sometimes called Cap Joli, Pretty Hill, by the voyageurs. To the B.C. Hydro and Power Authority it is affectionately known as Damsite X, with a flooding reserve to the "1000 foot contour".

Along the river a wide slash will sometimes be noticed on one bank, sometimes on both. These can be seismic trails or winter roads. Winter is the time when this muskeg country comes alive with exploration crews looking for gas and oil. Twenty km below the Butte is Francois, an old H.B.C. trading post, now marked with a red and white building and two cabins. Another 17 km and canoeists leave B.C. to enter the Northwest Territories.

The Liard is now extremely wide and the channel is often separated by large islands as much as 3 km across. To the left, Pointed Mountain and the Liard Range can be seen. Soon far ahead a cluster of buildings will be noticed on the right bank, enough to quicken the stroke of any tired paddler. Flags fly and probably people will come down to the floats to welcome you and canoeists will have a small idea what it is like to arrive at a wilderness outpost. This is Fort Liard. The White settlement consists of a nurse, an R.C.M.P. constable, a Forest Ranger, H.B.C. supervisor, a priest, a power plant operator and a couple of teachers.

The settlement is on the right bank at the confluence of the Liard and Petitot Rivers. Along the Petitot there is an Indian village of some size. This is a remnant of a previous century, one of fur traders, trappers, prospectors and explorers, men living on the brink of civilization. It is a place where one can still savour the feeling of one of the outposts.

Historically Fort Liard was established in 1800 by the H.B.C. and was the jumping off point for John MacLeod's exploration of the Dease Lake country, and later Robert Campbell's journeys into the Yukon.

Today the canoeist will either fly back to Fort Nelson or continue downstream to Nahanni Butte or Fort Simpson. If the latter route is chosen a complete description will be found in *Canoe Routes Yukon*. There are no major rapids between here and Nahanni. Flett Rapids present no problem. From Nahanni there is one set of Rapids to Fort Simpson, but they are easily passed. Below the Nahanni the river is wider yet and less interesting.

ROUTE - LIARD RIVER - FRANCES LAKE, Y.T. TO FORT SIMPSON, N.W.T.
Wild River

GRADE - *2 to 3, rapids to 5*
LENGTH - *1400 km, 6 to 12 portages*
WIDTH - *10 metres to 1.5 km*
VERTICAL DROP - *762 metres*
TIME TO ALLOW - *1 month*
NEAREST EMERGENCY COMMUNICATION - *Alaska Highway communities, Fort Liard, Nahanni Butte, Fort Simpson*
CAMPING - ACCOMMODATION - *Unorganized*
MAPS - *N.T.S. 1:250,000 105H, 105A, 104P, 94M, 94N, 94O, 95B, 95G, 95H*
HAZARDS - *Grade 5 to 6 rapids, arduous portages, remote, long*

DIRECTIONS

Put-in at Fraces Lake, north of Watson Lake on the Alaska Highway, and take-out at Fort Simpson on the Mackenzie River in the Northwest Territories.

DESCRIPTION

This river trip is one of the most historic, one of the longest, and one of the most difficult in Canada. It begins in the Yukon Territories, crosses northern B.C. and them empties into the Mackenzie River at Fort Simpson in the N.W.T. Few people have canoed it in recent years but there is a growing interest in its waters. Because it is usually considered a B.C. river we have given a brief mention of it in this volume. It is described in detail in *Canoe Routes Yukon*, as that is the beginning point of the trip. The lower portion of the river near Fort Liard is described as a continuation of the Fort Nelson River. Interior Canoe Outfitters in Kamloops run expeditions down the river each summer, providing a practical way for most people to make such a lengthy expedition.

ROUTE - GATAGA - KECHIKA RIVER *Wild River*
GRADE - *2 - 4 +*
LENGTH - *320 km, 4 to 8 portages*
WIDTH - *4.5 to 120 metres*
VERTICAL DROP - *697 metres, 2 metres per km*
TIME TO ALLOW - *10 to 14 days*
NEAREST EMERGENCY COMMUNICATION - *Fireside on Alaska Highway. Radio at Moor's outfitting camp, 16 km north of Gataga-Kechika confluence.*
CAMPING - ACCOMMODATION - *Unorganized*
MAPS - *N.T.S. 1:250,000 94K Tuchodi Lakes; 94L Kechika; 94M Rabbit River*
HAZARDS - *Remote, rapids, sweepers*

DIRECTIONS

Float plane only. Fly from Watson lake to an unnamed lake at 125 25' W 58 3' N on sheet 94K. Take-out at Skook's Landing on Liard River. Access from Alaska Highway.

DESCRIPTION

The South Gataga River has its headwaters in the northern peaks of the Rocky Mountains, running between the Rockies and the Kechika Range to the Kechika River. The Kechika flows north through the Rocky Mountain

Trench into the Liard River. The river valleys consist mainly of white spruce, with some poplar and cottonwood groves along the shore. Not far above are the alpine meadows with a wide variety of flowers, shrubs and mosses.

Wildlife along the route includes moose, stone sheep in the Kechika Mountains, caribou, mule deer, some elk, goats, grizzly, black bear, wolf, beaver, lynx and other furbearers. Birds include Canada geese, harlequin ducks, loons, gulls, hawks, grouse, ptarmigan, jays, ravens, terns, and a few shorebirds. There are pike and grayling in the rivers and rainbow and lake trout in the lakes.

Locals refer to the Kechika as the Muddy River, an indication of the silt that is carried downstream. Kechika is a Sikanni Indian word for "big windy", while Gataga means "white water", referring to the glacial silt washed down in the water.

This journey is obviously for those experienced in wilderness paddling, and preferably in good shape, for the first 9.5 km are extremely difficult. The Gataga is reached by following a small stream that exits the lake described in the directions. The stream is 12 km long, but only 2.5 km can be canoed. In the 9.5 km the stream drops 300 metres. In addition the first 6.5 km are covered in deadfall, and the lower stream has rapids and falls. Portage on the high ground where walking is a little easier. If you follow the south bank another stream will be reached which leads 3 km to the Gataga.

Where the small unnamed stream runs into the Gataga the river is 15 metres wide with a velocity of 9.5 km per hour. A set of rapids requiring scouting is 9.5 km downstream. A portage passes on the left bank, 90 metres long. If you run the rapid use the left side. Over the next 3 km the banks become higher and the standing waves larger as a gorge is approached. The gorge should be partially portaged as there are large boulders in a narrows just a few hundred metres downstream. A game trail on the left makes a good portage. Follow it to a small stream and then portage and line the stream for a kilometre back to the South Gataga. Although this is still in the gorge it can be easily run. The confluence with the Gataga is 11 km downstream.

From the confluence of the Gataga to the junction with the Kechika there are just two rapids. The first is 1.5 km past Through Creek, about 25 km downstream from the confluence. Here a large rock has formed two chutes which is best portaged by a 90 metre carry on the right, beginning on a sandy beach. The next rapid is 3 km further, but should not cause any problems. From here to the Kechika watch for a braided channel and a few log jams.

For the next 190 km there are few hazards to canoeing, though log-jams and resulting back eddies and boils should be watched for. There are also some sharp turns. Downstream 16 km from the Gataga Forks is Matulka Creek where a trail on the right leads to Moor's outfitting camp. There is a single-side band radio here in case of emergency. Another 24 km downstream is a small trading post. This is Skook Davidson's country, a man who became a legend in his own lifetime as a horseman and guide.

Fifty-six km below the post the Turnagain River flows in from the west. A small cabin with two bunks is 450 metres up the Turnagain on the north side. Downstream from this Fork the Kechika stays in a single channel until the current begins to increase 16 km above the Liard River. Over these last 16 km there are 8 sets of rapids. All can be paddled at high water, but be sure to scout them.

At the Liard River canoeists will have to paddle across to Skook's Landing, about 1 km downstream on the left bank of the Liard. It would be wise to paddle upstream a little first as the crossing allows no time for mistakes. Mountain Portage Rapids lie just a few metres below the landing. It is necessary to go behind an island and run one of two chutes caused by a large rock.

The Alaska Highway is just 360 metres away, and five kilometres north is Fireside, where limited services are available. *The Headless Valley* by Ranulph Fiennes describes a trek up the Kechika as part of a north south traverse of the province. It will provide additional information on the Kechika River.

ROUTE - FRASER - YELLOWHEAD CREEK TO TETE JAUNE CACHE
Recreational River

GRADE - *2*
LENGTH - *76 km, 1 portage of 29 km*
WIDTH - *30 metres*
VERTICAL DROP - *377 metres*
TIME TO ALLOW - *2 days*
NEAREST EMERGENCY COMMUNICATION - *Park Headquarters at Red Pass or Valemount*
CAMPING - ACCOMMODATION - *Provincial Parks campsite on Yellowhead Lake and at Robson Meadows*
MAPS - *N.T.S. 1:250,000 83D Canoe River; 83E Mount Robson; 93H McBride*
HAZARDS - *Swift cold water, some sweepers.*

DIRECTIONS

Take the Yellowhead Highway to Mount Robson Provincial Park. Put-in where Highway crosses the Fraser just west of Yellowhead Lake. Take-out at Red Pass, and portage to Rearguard Falls. Take-out 1 km below Highway 5 crossing, just below old Tête Jaune Bridge, on the left side.

DESCRIPTION

Although not the actual headwaters of the river this launching point on the Yellowhead Highway is the closest one can come without lining or portaging upstream. Some paddlers might prefer to start at Yellowhead Lake, but there is really little point as it is not the headwaters of the Fraser. The river begins some 40 km to the south at the base of the Rocky Mountains.

From there the river flows 1368 km in a giant curve to flow into the Pacific Ocean at Vancouver. In its course it drains over 146,500 square km. It is named for Simon Fraser, an explorer with the Northwest Company, who on May 22, 1808 set out from what was to become Fort George to explore this then unknown waterway. His journey to the Pacific and back was one of the most daring ever to take place in Canada.

This section of river to Tête Jaune Cache was not used by early travellers. A trail lead through the Yellowhead pass to Tête Jaune Cache and for various periods of time provided a route to Kamloops and Tête Jaune, and ultimately Fort George. River travel though was reserved for the section below Tête Jaune. During railway construction Yellowhead and Moose Lakes were used by barges freighting supplies, but canoes were seldom if ever seen. Today however it is an interesting route on its own, or for paddlers wanting to travel the whole river.

Fishing in this part of the Fraser is good for Dolly Varden and rainbow once the river has cleared after about July 1st. Wildlife along the route includes, bears, deer, moose, wolves, coyotes and beaver. Birds likely to be seen are the dipper or water ouzel, harlequins, Canada geese and songbirds.

From the launching point there is about 16 km of Grade 2 water with one bridge crossing the river at the 5 km point. This is followed by 8 km of grade 1 river and then the 13 km of Moose Lake. Moose River flows in on the right near the head of the lake and a short hike upstream will lead to Moose Falls, not seen from the lake or highway. During railway construction Moose City was built on the shore, a trans-shipping point for barges. Canoeists who brought their diving gear might like to dive for one of the lost cargoes, a load of rum kegs that was searched for by many a thirsty gandy dancer.

Across Moose Lake is Rainbow Falls, tumbling down the left side from the high ridge. Dolly Varden to 9 kilograms and Lake trout to 18 kilograms have been caught in the lake.

At the end of Moose Lake is Red Pass station. Take-out here and portage to below Rearguard Falls. Sections of the river between here and there are navigable but drops like Overlander Falls and Rearguard Falls, plus several others with difficult portages make the route impractical. This is probably the reason the route was not used historically.

Below Rearguard Falls, which marks the limit of the upward migration of salmon, there is 5 km of grade 2 water to Tête Jaune Cache. Pull-out just downstream of a small canyon, below the new bridge and below the old trestle bridge to Tête Jaune Cache. There is a clearing on the left bank that was the site of frequent camps of Indians and travellers that can still be used.

ROUTE - FRASER RIVER - TETE JAUNE TO PRINCE GEORGE *Recreational River*
GRADE - *1, rapids grade 2 to 5*
LENGTH - *444 km, 1 portage*
WIDTH - *30 to 150 metres*

VERTICAL DROP - *183 metres*

TIME TO ALLOW - *1 week*

NEAREST EMERGENCY COMMUNICATION - *Settlements with telephones at: Tête Jaune, Dunster, McBride, Crescent Spur, Dome Creek, Penny, McGregor, Shelley and Prince George*

CAMPING - ACCOMMODATION - *Unorganized*

MAPS - *N.T.S. 1:250,000 93H McBride; 93I Monkman Pass; 93J McLeod Lake; 93G Prince George*

HAZARDS - *Some sweepers and snags, grade 5 rapids at Grand Canyon*

DIRECTIONS

Tête Jaune is at the junction of Yellowhead 5 and 16. Put-in at the take-out described for the upper Fraser Section. Take-out at any road access or Fort George Park in Prince George.

DESCRIPTION

Canoeists wanting to travel an easy section of the Fraser would do well to consider the segment from Tête Jaune to Penny. For 240 km the river flows in large meander bends past old mill sites, settlements on backwater meanders, homesteads and trappers cabins. This is all grade 1 water except for the Goat River Rapids which are grade 2. Below Penny however the river surges through the Grand Canyon of the Fraser, a piece of water that has taken over a hundred lives. Most of these were early travellers and freighters who were running unwieldy craft and who could not swim.

157

The Indians who inhabited the upper Fraser did not use it to any great extent for transportation. They hunted along the valley and traditionally camped at Tête Jaune during the salmon migration but really knew little of the river. In the early 1800's the Hudson's Bay Company used the river as a connecting link between Jasper House and Fort George, but use was spasmodic and no regular route was established. The Overlanders were the next large group to use the river. They arrived at Tête Jaune on August 21st 1862, after having spent three months on the trail from Fort Garry, now Winnipeg. At Tête Jaune they had to decide how to continue. One small group split off and went south through the Thompson country but the larger party of approximately 130 decided to travel the Fraser. They built a variety of craft, ranging from "20 x 40 foot" log rafts to Indian dugouts and even a bull boat fashioned from ox hides.

During the construction of the Grand Trunk Pacific, railway supplies and construction materials were rafted down the Fraser on barges which were then dismantled downstream and used for building materials. The trip was easy and pleasant except for the Grand Canyon and here many of the men lost their lives. Sternwheelers used the river for two short years, being stopped by the construction of a low bridge at Dome Creek. Since that time the river has seen a few homesteaders, trappers and hunters in a variety of craft. Modern canoeists paddle in the wake of these people.

From Tête Jaune the route passes a number of other rivers, and a few settlements where telephones and road access are available. Dunster is a farm community above the river at km 45 where the river is crossed by a small bridge. At km 84 the town of McBride is passed and again there is a bridge crossing the river. Below here is a traditional caribou migration route. Watch for them along the river, particularly in the fall months.

Goat River flows in from the left at km 135 and a few km below are the Goat River rapids, usually passed unnoticed. There is a stretch of fast water that sternwheelers had trouble with in certain water levels. Downstream another few km, at 151 km is Crescent Spur, once a large lumber town but now inhabited by only a few people who work at a small mill. There are no services here.

Dome Creek, at km 208, is another farm community with few services but there are telephones should you need one, and it is certainly an interesting place to spend a few hours. The railway bridge that crosses here, called Mile 145 by the railway, was the one that blocked the sternwheelers upstream travel and resulted in court cases trying to have it removed. A tent town grew on the left bank, upstream of the bridge during construction days. The town was simply called Mile 145.

Penny is a town on the right bank of the river, reached by railway only. There is an access road on the left however where cars are left and boats taken to the town. The road leads approximately 5 km to the Yellowhead Highway. Paddlers who do not want to tackle the Grand Canyon of the Fraser should take out here.

The history and natural history of this area is described in *Yellowhead Mileposts* Volume II, by the authors of this book.

The Grand Canyon is 40 km below Penny. The water here can reach Grade 5. The Canyon consists of two narrow guts through volcanic rock, the first constricting the water to a quarter of its normal width. Sternwheelers with engines going full speed astern raced through at "15 miles per hour" it is told. Art Downs in his book *Paddlewheels on the Frontier* quotes a travellers description on the second section. It was a "cavernous opening scarcely fifty feet wide, presenting a specter of somber, awful grandeur. It was like peering into a huge vault..." At the mouth of this gut was a whirlpool that swallowed trees and on occasion men and rafts. One Overlander disappeared here, and in the first few weeks of the freighting season of 1913 over 20 men were drowned and goods totalling over $100,000 were lost.

At 320 km, 40 km below the canyon, the Hansard Bridge is passed. This bridge carries rail and automobile traffic and leads to the town of McGregor, on the left right bank. The road on the left gives road access to Prince George. At 368 km Giscome Canyon is run, with no difficulty. At 388 km the Giscome Rapids are reached, a 6 km stretch of grade 2 water.

Below here is clear paddling to the city of Prince George at 444 km. An appropriate spot to land would be the reconstructed Fort George, located just downstream from the confluence of the Nechako and the Fraser.

ROUTE - FRASER RIVER - PRINCE GEORGE TO HOPE *Recreational River*
GRADE - *1 to 2 with rapids 3 to 6*
LENGTH - *592 km, many portages may be necessary*
WIDTH - *30 metres to 250 metres*
VERTICAL DROP - *527 metres*
TIME TO ALLOW - *10 day to 2 weeks*
NEAREST EMERGENCY COMMUNICATION - *Prince George, Quesnel, Soda Creek, Lillooet, Lytton, various Fraser Canyon communities, Yale, Hope, reaction ferries at Marguerite, Big Bar and Stein River; highway at Sheep Creek Crossing*
CAMPING - ACCOMMODATION - *Unorganized; good locations on river banks and bars*
MAPS - *N.T.S. 1:250,000 93G Prince George; 93B Quesnel; 920 Taseko Lakes; 92P Bonaparte River; 1:126,720 921/NW Ashcroft; 921/SW Lytton; 92H/NW Yale; 92H/SW Chilliwack*
HAZARDS - *Large water volumes, turbulence, rapids to grade 6 some driftwood; Water not safe to drink; Strenuous portages at some water levels*

DIRECTIONS

Put-in at Fort George Park in Prince George. Take-out is possible at any of the many communities or road accesses along the route. Take-out in Hope just below the Highway bridge on the left side.

DESCRIPTION

This segment of the Fraser has seen much more development than the upstream portions. Fraser explored it first in 1808, travelling the river in both directions. Canoeists contemplating this journey should read his journal as it gives one of the best descriptions available. With a copy of his book, good topo sheets and some scouting, paddlers should have no trouble recognizing rapids and canyons and being prepared for them. Fraser's journal and letters have been edited by W. Kaye Lamb and published by Macmillan.

Paddlers must recognize that paddling the Fraser is unlike any other trip in the province. The large volumes of water create turbulence, boils, eddies and whirlpools on what is still classed as grade 1 or 2 water. These hydraulics can quickly and easily flip a canoe and drown the occupants. The speed of the river varies from 6 to 13 km per hour with water volumes increasing tenfold from low to high water. Rapids and canyons are constantly changing. In low water the canyons may be flat water and in high water have turbulence that cannot possibly be run. High water may wash out other rapids enough to make them non-existent, yet in low water they may have waves and souse holes that will swallow canoes. This is not a river for novice paddlers. Scout ahead at all times and keep your life jacket on.

From Prince George to Soda Creek, the route formerly taken by sternwheelers, the river is grade 1 to 2, with the exception of two canyons. Red Rock or Fort George Canyon is located 20 km downstream of Prince George. The grade 3 to 5 rapids here can be skirted on the left side of the river. Cottonwood Canyon, 5 km upstream of the Cottonwood River, are grade 3 to 4. Depending on water levels there will be a route through the centre or along the left side. There is an old gold mine on the left bank at the downstream end of the canyon.

The Cottonwood River flows in from the left and then a large meander bend leads to Quesnel where there is easy access to the river. The Quesnel River flows in here.

From Quesnel to Soda Creek is straight - forward canoeing. There is a reaction ferry at Marguerite and many ranches and farms bordering the river. Near Soda Creek Rudy Johnson's bridge crosses the river. Just beyond Soda Creek is Whiskey Creek and then **Williams** Lake River flows in from the left.

At Soda Creek the easy ride is over as the Fraser now enters canyon country that lasts until Hope. Each section of rough water or canyon should be scouted ahead as on some there is no turning back once a canoe has entered. Portages may be difficult and long. From Soda Creek to Lillooet there is very little river access and the country is considerably drier and warmer than upstream. As the river between rapids is standard we will list only the rapids and their location.

Soda Creek Canyon, 1 km below the site of Soda Creek. Rapids to grade 3 or 4. Can sometimes be run in open decked canoes. Portaging or lining may be necessary.

Chimney Creek Canyon, so named for a butte at the creeks mouth, is a narrow passsage with steep walls, grade 3. Sneak by on the left or line along the same side.

Doc English Gulch Rapids are 8 km below Sheep Creek Bridge. Portage or line along the right shore. These may be what are erroneously called Iron Rapids on Topo sheets. Where Iron Rapids are marked there are no rapids of any kind. At low water this may be passable.

Portage du Baril is grade 3 in low water and 4 in highwater. Fraser and his party portaged this rough rapid, with some difficulty. "And at this end, when everything was brought over," he wrote, "we tapped our small keg of shrub (a mixture of fruit juice, sugar and rum) which induced us to call this Portage de Barriel and gave all hands a dram." The portage is on the left just above the canyon. It is approximately 1 km in length.

Meason Creek Rapids occur just below the junction with the Chilcotin that flows in from the right. There is some tricky water here and a large eddy that even large inflatables can get caught in. The difference in height between the eddy and the main river may be as much as a metre. Portage along the left shore.

Gaspard Creek Rapids consist of 2 metre waves and tongue formations caused by the narrowing of the river. These are grade 3 in low water. Portage may be taken along the right side, across Gaspard Creek. Downstream a few km is the bridge to Gang Ranch. There is a take-out on the left bank just below the bridge, used by rafters as it has good road access. On the right Churn Creek flows in. The delta was a logging operation and may be a good place to camp.

Below this point there are several grade 3 chutes in places like Canoe Creek, China Gulch Canyon, and Lone Cabin Creek. These are easily skirted in most water levels.

Rapid Couvert or French Bar Canyon is 2 km upstream from the Big Bar Ferry. Here the river runs over a series of ledges and then becomes constricted in a narrow gorge. In low water there are considerable large waves and souse holes where the river flows over ledges. In high water the water is backed up by the gorge, washing out the ledges and forming great turbulence at the mouth. It can be scouted and portaged over the right bank. The portage is about 3 km long and difficult. Elevation gained is about 213 metres.

Big Bar Ferry is a good place for paddlers to pull out. The road from the ferry leads to Clinton, or over a rough road on the right, to Lillooet. The river below here is not suitable for canoes. The Moran Canyon between here and Lillooet has 15 canyons and/or rapids, several of which are grade 4 or greater. The river is only about 30 metres wide in spots. It should be run only by large inflatables with an experienced crew. The last section of the canyon is the Bridge River Rapid. Here even the commercial rafting companies prefer to portage all their gear and passengers. They can be portaged on the right bank along the road.

Canoes must take-out at Big Bar Ferry. There are no commercial bus or truck lines from Big Bar. Vehicle pickup must be pre-arranged.

Put-in again at Lillooet, a town with all services. The easiest river and vehicle access is at Cayoosh Park at the mouth of the Seton River. From Lillooet to Lytton the river is not difficult though there are some grade 2 and 3 chutes that will have to be avoided by sneaking along the side. There is one set of rapids that is grade 4 just downstream of Cinquefoil Creek which flows in on the left. A portage may be necessary here.

Downstream of Lytton the obstacles increase as there are several small rapids in the 44 km to Boston Bar. Most are grade 2 to 3 and can be skirted on one side or the other. Those that require scouting are a narrows 500 metres above the C.N.R. railway bridge. Scout carefully. A portage is possible along the left side using the railway grade. At Kanaka Bar there is another set of rapids that should be scouted between the bar and Kwoiek Creek. Ainslee Creek is another spot that must be scouted. Portage along the left bank. This whole section of river is such that scouting should become second nature.

The Fraser from Boston Bar south to Yale is extremely difficult. Canoeists should not attempt it unless they are expert with at least decked canoes. Scouting will take up a large amount of the travel time as there are several major rapids. Portaging will definitely be necessary. The river here is confined to the canyon which makes scouting and portaging difficult. The rapids also change greatly depending on water levels. In high water some rapids will disappear, while others will appear at the downstream side of any constraining feature. In the canyons of this section the water level varies as much as 30 metres between high and low water. It can change 3 metres overnight. There are 6 major rapids in the 42 km.

Skuzzy Rapids actually begin a kilometre above China Bar where the river makes a hard turn. This and Skuzzy are best portaged along the right side, using the railway grade.

Between there and Hell's Gate there may be canoeable sections. Some will prefer to keep on carrying, crossing the river on the Hell's Gate bridge. This section must be portaged. Cross the river to the left side and continue downstream to a steep slope that leads to the river.

Little Hell's Gate may have to be portaged. That is certainly safest. Scout and portage along the right.

Black Canyon is next and reaches grade 4. Scout before running. A portage may be necessary. There is fast and tricky water below this to the old Alexandria bridge.

At low water there may be rapids at the mouth of Spuzzum Creek. This would make seven major rapids.

Sailor Bar rapids are grade 4, sometime 5. Portage along the right shore.

Saddle Rock is an extremely difficult section. Waves here can reach 10 metres in height and have been known to swallow 24 foot inflatables. It is grade 4 to 6. Portage along the left side.

At highwater another rapid will appear at Lady Franklin Rock. A portage can be made along the right side, following the old Cariboo road.

From Yale the river starts to wind down. There are some whirlpools 1.5 km south of Yale at the mouth of Gordon Creek, and a grade 3 chute near Emory Creek mouth. Take the right side. Portage on the right if necessary. This is the last distinct rapid of the Fraser. But don't relax too much. Hope is now 16 km south. Relatively easy canoeing from here. Take-out on the left bank just below the highway bridge. All services are available in town which is right on the river.

ROUTE - FRASER RIVER - HOPE TO NEW WESTMINSTER
Recreational River
GRADE - *1*
LENGTH - *137 km*
WIDTH - *200 to 300 metres*
VERTICAL DROP - *40 metres*
TIME TO ALLOW - *1 to 3 days*
NEAREST EMERGENCY COMMUNICATION - *Hope, Mission, Fort Langley, Haney*
CAMPING - ACCOMMODATION - *Unorganized*
MAPS - *N.T.S. 1:250,000 92H/SW Chilliwack; 92G/SE Langley*
HAZARDS - *Floating debris and river traffic, water not safe to drink*

DIRECTIONS

Put-in at Hope underneath the highway bridge, on the left side. Take-out at New Westminster on right in dock area near old railway station.

DESCRIPTION

This lower part of the Fraser is used as the route of a race held every May 21st weekend and sponsored by the Hyack Festival Society of New Westminster. Winners make the trip in about 8 hours, but you would be wise to consider a little longer journey.

Waterfowl and small mammals are quite common along the route and in places the shores are still natural enough to feel you have escaped the rush of the freeway which is so close. In many spots the river has split into a number of channels and the route taken will depend on the paddlers interest. Other rivers such as the Harrison can be explored on the way and short portages will lead to a myriad of streams and sloughs that have been blocked off behind dykes.

Obstacles and hazards on the river are few. There is a permanent boom across 10 km below Hope, but a gate is located close to the south shore.

There are a number of easily seen road accesses and bridges near and across the river throughout the trip. Novice canoeists should beware of the immense volume of water that is now flowing beneath their small craft and care must be taken to avoid large eddies or boils. Near New Westminster large freighters, tugs, barges and a variety of power boats can make waves that will swamp canoes. Give them a wide berth. Do not drink the water of the Fraser as it is an open sewer for much of its course.

APPENDIX 1

Glossary

Air lock - Air space under an overturned canoe causing a suction which makes the canoe difficult to turn upright.
Back ferry - Move a canoe sideways while going downstream by back paddling with the canoe at an angle to the current.
Bar - Deposits of sand and rock in a creek or river, frequently near its mouth.
Beam - Width of a boat at its widest point.
Bilge - Interior of a boat below its waterline.
Blade - Flat section of a canoe paddle.
Boulder garden - Many boulders in a rapid requiring maneuvering to navigate.
Bow - Front end of a boat.
Bracket - Support for an outboard motor on a canoe.
Broach - Turn broadside to wind and waves.
Carry - A portage, where canoe and gear are carried around an obstruction or between navigable waterways; usually avoided by canoeists whenever possible!
Chute - Narrow channel between obstructions with faster water than adjacent current.
Closed canoe - Sometimes called a decked or slalom canoe, these are completely decked with cockpits fore and aft; paddlers sometimes wear spray skirts to seal cockpits; sometimes used for touring.
Deck - Small triangular section at bow and stern of canoe.
Decked canoe - Same as a closed canoe.
Draw stroke - Technique of moving a canoe sideways toward the paddle.
Eddy - A place where the current stops, or flows upstream; found along shorelines, inside of bends or behind obstructions.
Feather - To turn the paddle so that it moves through the air or water edgeways.
Ferry - To move a boat sideways across a current.
Flat water - Lake or slow water with no rapids.
Freeboard - Height of canoe above the waterline.
Freighter - Large canoe "over 18 feet in length" used to transport goods.
Gradient - The slope or drop in a river.
Grip - Top end of a canoe paddle that is shaped for holding.
Gunwale - Strips along topsides of canoe between bow and stern; prounced "gunnel", the name comes from the gun walls on early ships.
Haystack - Pile of water formed as fast moving water meets still water.
Heavy water - Large volume flow of turbulent water.
Hole - Hollow area caused by a reversal of current.
Kayak - Decked watertight craft styled after an Eskimo canoe.
Keel - Strip running from stem to stern along the bottom of a canoe.
Ledge - Ridge of rock that acts as a natural dam; difficult to see from water level.
Lee - Area of water or land sheltered from the wind.
Left bank - Left side of a river when facing downstream; the right side when facing upstream.
Lining - Using a rope to guide a canoe downstream; easier than portaging.
Open Canadian - Traditional canoe which does not have closed decking.
Painter - Rope used for holding or towing, attached to bow and or stern; the word is from the Old English panter or noose, Old French pantiere, snare, and/or Greek pantheros, catching every beast.
Poling - Moving a canoe by means of a pole; very effective in shallow water with a good bottom.
Portage - Carrying of canoe and gear around an obstruction or between navigable waterways; or the place where this is necessary.
Rapid - Swift flowing water with obstructions causing turbulence.
Reversal - Change in direction of current which turns back on itself; dangerous to get caught in.
Ribs - Curved strips of wood on a wood and canvas canoe, which run from gunwale to gunwale forming the framework of the canoe.
Riffle - Shallow rapid.
Right bank - Right side of a river when facing downstream; the left side when facing upstream.

Scout - Check out a rapid or part of the river from shore before running it; when in doubt, scout.

Slalom - An artificial course set up for competition, usually zig-zagging through rapids.

Sleeper - Submerged rock or obstacle hidden below the surface of the water.

Smoker - Extremely violent rapid.

Souse hole - Depression downriver of an underwater obstruction;where you get soused as the water rushes over the sides of the hole!

Spray cover - Temporary fabric cover used on open canoes in white water.

Standing wave - Wave of water which stays in position as water passes through, caused when fast moving water meets still water.

Stern - Rear end of a boat; the blunt end on a V stern.

Thwart - Cross brace on a canoe running from gunwale to gunwale.

Tracking - Using a rope to tow a canoe upstream.

Tumpline - Headstrap for carrying pack or canoe so that weight is transferred to the neck muscles; difficult and tiring for novices.

Windward - Direction from which the wind is blowing.

Yoke - Wide centre thwart carved or moulded to fit over shoulders and around neck when portaging a canoe.

The Outdoor Camera and Water

Our increased dependence on mechanical transportation for general use seems to have prompted a comparable parallel increase in the use of non-mechanical transportation for recreation. The energy crisis has made us all more aware of dwindling resources, and the need to use rapid transit and car pools in daily commuting kindles a desire to seek out the basics once again. Winter has seen a boom in cross-country skiing and summer a renewed interest in Canada's most historic method of transportation, the canoe. Coupled closely with this free energy downriver transportation has been a similar growth in the sports of kayaking and white-water rafting. Less than five years ago rafting was restricted to a few rivers like the Colorado, now it has spread to rivers all across North America.

Too often it is thought that water and cameras don't mix, and whenever a boat of any kind is approached cameras are kept safe inside a waterproof case, or left on shore. This protects the cameras of course, but photos will be disappointing. The challenge is to take photos and keep your cameras dry, in that order. With a few precautions and some advance planning both are possible.

Be sure your photo equipment is insured for all perils, so that wet, lost or stolen it will be covered. Some policies only protect against theft. Secondly you should have a strong waterproof case for film and extra equipment storage. The least expensive yet most indestructible containers are ammunition boxes, usually available from war surplus stores for a few dollars. A small one, about the size of a lunch kit, would hold two SLR's with either a few rolls of film, or an extra lens and a light meter. The largest will hold more equipment than most of us can afford. Two small ones, lined with foam and painted white to reflect heat, will make a good outfit. Test them in a tub or bucket and use them in rough water or anytime you are afraid of dunking. Canoeists can fasten one to the deck just in front of the kneeling pad. It may be left open when not in use but quickly closed. Cases should be tied to a thwart or seat with a line. Another method of waterproofing is to place cases or gadget bags in large reinforced plastic bags sold to hold canoe gear, or in war surplus de-lousing bags. However, these methods only keep cameras dry when they are not in use.

The ultimate in protection while shooting is an underwater housing, frequently awkward to use, or an underwater camera, though both of these are expensive and rather specialized. With either your problem of a wet camera is over. Otherwise it is often enough to simply lift the camera above your head when a wave approaches, or shield it under a life jacket. Another effective method is to wear the camera around your neck and keep a small plastic bag in one hand, into which the camera is dropped when the going gets rough. I have found this effective in all but the roughest water while rafting, but it is difficult to paddle with one hand. Barring all these precautions use your camera to take the best photos possible and hope that it doesn't get wet.

There may come a time when your precautions are not enough and your equipment takes a dunking. Recommended procedure is to keep the camera wet, to delay rusting, and rush it to a repair shop. If dropped in salt water rinse the camera in fresh water, then keep it wet. Either way it will have to be completely stripped and cleaned. Beware of a quote that only involves cleaning or minimal dismantling as it could mean later trouble. Should the camera not get completely soaked you will have to decide if it needs repair. Ideally it should have the same treatment as if it were dunked. If it was only splashed you may be able to do enough with a towel and a can of compressed air. It is still advisable to have it checked out. Should you be a long way from repair, and need your camera, you may be able to use it by drying thoroughly and carefully lubricating some moving parts. I once kept a movie camera operating this way for a week after it spent 20 minutes under the rapids of the Chilko River.

Exposed wet film need not be thrown out. Send it to the lab with a note explaining what happened. Sometimes it can be saved. If you can do your own processing within hours keep the film moist and carefully unroll it in the darkroom. If it will be days before processing you can try unrolling it in the dark and drying the film, or let it dry on the spool and then soak it carefully before processing. You should be able to save at least some frames this way.

Lens choice for canoe tripping or white-water photography depends on the type of expedition and the photos you want. For instance shots of the canoe you are paddling will require a 28mm or wider, but this will be a little too wide for photos of nearby boats. A 35mm, 50mm or 105mm would be a good choice for photos of accompanying canoes, or people. When shooting from shore try some wide angle shots showing the country and scenery around the waterway, and telephoto shots, ie. 300mm to 500mm for closeups of the canoes. Zoom lenses are also a good choice, mainly because equipment is vulnerable to accidents when an equipment case is open to change lenses or film.

As in any type of photography a certain amount of practice is needed before consistently good, well exposed, exciting photos are produced. You will have to learn what lenses are best, where to take an exposure reading, the most effective shutter speeds and what angles work well. If you want to shoot other canoes, kayaks or rafters scout the location ahead of time. Determine which side of the river has the sun and where canyon shadows will be. Low angles will accentuate waves, a necessity as they always appear smaller from shore, and telephotos will stack up water and canoes to make rapids seem much more ominous than with a wide angle. High angles tend to show the craft and its occupants better. Shutter speeds should be fast, 1/250th and up, to stop most action, but it would be a good idea to try some slow speeds, such as 1/30th, to impart a feeling of motion.

Canoeists who become more interested in photography should try taking a trip where someone else does most of the work, even the paddling, for photography takes skill, time and concentration, as does paddling, and it is difficult to do both at the same time and be effective.

One good place to practice white-water photography is at a kayak race where man and boat are one with the river. Scout the course ahead of time to locate various gates and anticipate action. Perhaps there is a gate that must be run in reverse, a large rock and souse hold that experts will take to save precious seconds, or a bad rapid that is sure to bring on upsets. All of these can be shot from the dry safety of shore and will be excellent practice for the time when you want to photograph on your own expedition.

Canoe-tripping and water is an ideal photographic subject and needs only a little advance planning and a few precautions to become one of the most effective means of reliving a canoe trip. For the photographer it can become one of the most exhilarating and rewarding experiences and subjects you are likely to find. So on your next canoe journey down one of these routes make a camera part of your equipment, and record the trip on your own time machine.

APPENDIX 3

Canoe Clubs

Alberni Valley Paddlers c/o 734 Brown Road, Port Alberni
Beaver Canoe Club c/o #704A - 7360 Halifax, Burnaby
Burnaby Aquatic Club 2636 East 22 Avenue, Vancouver
Burnaby Canoe Club c/o 636 Tyndale, Coquitlam
Burquitlam Kayak and Canoe Club 636 Tyndale Street, Coquitlam
Coureur de Bois Canoe Club Box 317, Oliver
Dogwood Canoe Club P.O. Box 80748, Burnaby
Horsefly Canoe Club Box 21, Horsefly
Kamloops Canoe Club Box 812, Kamloops
Northwest Brigade Canoe Club Box 327, Prince George
Oak Bay Senior Secondary School Canoe Club, 2151 Cranmore Road, Victoria
Port Moody Canoe Club Box 41, 2881 Barnet Hwy., Port Moody
Salmon Arm Canoe Club Box 1245, Salmon Arm
Simon Fraser Outdoor Club S.F.U., Burnaby
Terrace Canoe Club c/o Recreation Director, 3215 Eby Street, Terrace
U.B.C. Kayak and Canoe Club Box 17, Student Union Building, U.B.C., Vancouver
Vancouver Kayak and Canoe Club 3519 Point Grey Road, Vancouver
Vernon Canoe Club Box 1241, Vernon
Victoria Canoe and Kayak Club Box 1552, Victoria
Wander Paddlers of B.C. c/o 724 Poplar Street, Coquitlam

APPENDIX 4

Canoe and Whitewater Instruction

Outdoor Recreation Department Capilano College, 2055 Purcell Way, North Vancouver,
V7J 3H5 (986-1911)
Similkameen Wilderness Centre Box 356, Keremeos, V0X 1N0 (499-2093)
Interior Canoe Outfitters Ltd. 751 Athabasca East, Kamloops, V2H 1C7 (743-9434)
Canoe Sport B.C. 1200 Hornby St., Vancouver, V6Z 2E2 (687-3333)
Kanawa Expeditions 1-2245 Trafalger, Vancouver, V6K 3S8 (731-2033)
John Hatchard - Tynke Braaksma 12-149 West 19th St., North Vancouver, V7M 1X3
(987-3879)
Outward Bound 1616 West 7th Ave., Vancouver, V6J 1S5 (733-9014)
Wright's River Explorations 549 Ioco Road, Port Moody, V3H 2W3 (461-6361)

Whitewater Tours

River Outfitters Association of British Columbia 1200 Hornby St., Vancouver, V6Z 2E2
(687-3333)
Canadian River Expeditions Ltd. 845 Chilco St., Vancouver, V6G 2R2 (926-4436)
Canyon Voyager 7268 14th Ave., Burnaby, V3N 1Z4 (526-8924)
Kumsheen Raft Adventures Ltd. Lytton, V0K 1Z0 (455-2410)
Safari River Expeditions Ltd. 969 West Broadway, Vancouver, V5Z 1K3 (738-5917)
Thompson Guiding Ltd. Riske Creek, V0L 1T0 (659-5635)
Westwater Adventures Ltd. 6100 Mara Crescent, Richmond, V7C 2P9 (277-5753)
John Hatchard - Tynke Braaksma 12-149 West 19th St., North Vancouver, V7M 1X3
(987-3879)
Whitewater Adventures Ltd. Box 46536, Vancouver, V6H 4G8 (879-6701)
Wright's River Explorations 549 Ioco Road, Port Moody, V3H 2W3 (461-6361)

APPENDIX 5

Canoe and Water Races

The time schedule and sometimes the location of races will vary from year to year. The races listed here will give an idea of competitions that have been held as well as locale and approximate time of year.

Annual B.C. High School Canoe Regatta, Chase - June
Annual Horsefly River Canoe Race, Horsefly - July
Annual Kettle River Raft Race - July
Annual Telkwa to Smithers Bulkley River Canoe Races - August
Annual Vedder River Raft Race - Abbotsford - June
Big Dam Canoe Race, Fort St. John - August
Columbia River Days Canoe Race, Revelstoke - August
Fraser Lake Canoe Race, Fraser Lake - July
Hyack Canoe Marathon, Hope to New Westminster, Langley to New Westminster - May
Labatt Whitewater Classic, Smithers - August
Mission to Maple Ridge Raft Race - May
Overlander Days Raft Race, Clearwater to Kamloops - July
Simon Fraser Canoe Marathon, Burnaby - September
Vanderhoof Canoe Race, Vanderhoof - July
Victoria Canoe Club Gorge Race, Victoria - September

BIBLIOGRAPHY

Books

Adney, Edwin Tappan & Howard I. Chapelle, **The Bark Canoes and Skin Boats of North America,** Smithsonian Institution, Washington, D.C., 1964

Akrigg, G.P.V. & Helen B., **1001 British Columbia Place Names,** Discovery Press, Vancouver, 1973

Balf, Mary, **Kamloops, A History of the District up to 1914,** Kamloops Museum, Kamloops, 1969

Barz, Crowley, Crowley & Wharton, **Trails to the Shuswap,** Shuswap Outdoors, Salmon Arm, 1976

Canoe Sport British Columbia, **British Columbia Canoe Routes,** Nunaga Publishing Company (now Antonson Publishing Ltd.,) Surrey, 1974, (out of print)

Corner, John, **Pictographs in the Interior of B.C.,** 1968

Davidson, James West and John Rugge, **The Complete Wilderness Paddler,** Alfred A. Knopf, New York, 1976

Department of Recreation and Conservation, **British Columbia Recreational Atlas,** Department of Recreation and Conservation, Victoria

Disley, John, **Orienteering,** Stackpole Books, 1973

Downs, Art, **Paddlewheels on the Frontier,** Foremost Publishing Co. Ltd., Surrey, 1967

Fear, Gene, **Surviving the Unexpected Wilderness Emergency,** Survival Education Association, Tacoma, Washington, 1975

Fraser, Simon, **Letters & Journals 1806-1808,** Edited by W. Kaye Lamb, Macmillan, Toronto, 1960

Hobson, Richmond P., Jr., **Grass Beyond the Mountains,** J.B. Lippincott Company, New York, 1951, **Nothing Too Good for a Cowboy,** J.B. Lippincott Company, New York, 1955, **The Rancher Takes a Wife,** Longmans, Green & Company, Toronto, 1961

Huser, Verne, **River Running,** Henry Regnery Company, Chicago, 1975

Hutchinson, Bruce, **The Fraser,** Clarke, Irwin & Company Limited, Toronto, Vancouver, 1965

Jenkinson, Michael, **Wild Rivers of North America,** E.P. Dutton & Company, Inc., New York, 1973

Kjellstrom, Bjorn, **Be Expert with Map & Compass,** Revised, Charles Schribner & Sons, 1967

Lathrop, Theodore, **Hypothermia, Killer of the Unprepared,** Leon R. Greenman, 1970

Mackenzie, Alexander, **Voyages from Montreal on the River St. Laurence through the Continent of North America,** M.G. Hartig Ltd., Edmonton, 1971

Malo, John W., **Wilderness Canoeing,** Collier Books, New York, 1971

McDonald, Archibald, **Peace River,** A canoe voyage from Hudson's Bay to the Pacific, by the late Sir George Simpson; in 1828, Coles Publishing Company, Toronto, 1970

McGinnis, William, **Whitewater Rafting,** Quadrangle/The New York Times Book Co., New York, 1975

McNair, Robert E., **Basic River Canoeing,** American Camping Association, Inc., Martinsville, Indiana, 1969

Morse, Eric W., **Fur Trade Canoe Routes of Canada/Then and Now,** Queen's Printer, Ottawa, 1969

Nickels, Nick, **Canoe Canada,** Van Nostrand Reinhold Ltd., Toronto, 1976

Olson, Sigurd F., **Listening Point,** Alfred A. Knopf, New York, 1966

Patterson, R.M., **For Pastures,** Gray's Publishing, Sidney, 1963, **Finlay's River,** Macmillan of Canada, Toronto, 1968, **The Dangerous River,** Gray's Publishing Ltd., Sidney, 1966, **Trail to the Interior,** William Morrow & Co. Inc., New York, 1966

Riviere, Bill, **Pole, Paddle & Portage, A complete Guide to Canoeing,** Van Nostrand Reinhold Company, New York, 1969

Sierra Club of British Columbia, **The West Coast Trail and Nitinat Lakes,** Douglas & McIntyre, Vancouver, 1980

Stewart, Dave, **Exploring British Columbia Waterways,** Southern Interior Lakes - Rivers - Streams, Saltaire Publishing Ltd., Sidney, 1976

Stowe, Leland, **Crusoe of Lonesome Lake,** Random House, New York, 1957

Thompson, David, **Travels in Western North America 1784 - 1812,** Edited by Victor G. Hopwood, Macmillan of Canada, Toronto, 1971

Underhill, J.E. (Ted), **Wild Berries of the Pacific Northwest,** Superior Publishing Company, Seattle, 1974

Walker, T.A. (Tommy), **Spatsizi,** Nunaga Publishing Company (now Antonson Publishing Ltd.,) Surrey, 1976

Wright, Richard & Rochelle, **Canoe Routes Yukon Territory,** Douglas & McIntyre, Vancouver, 1980

Wright, Richard & Rochelle, **Cariboo Mileposts,** Mitchell Press, Vancouver, 1972 **Yellowhead Mileposts,** Mitchell Press, Vancouver, 1974, 1977

Booklets, Pamphlets & Reports

Beware of Hypothermia, B.C. Department of Recreation and Conservation, Victoria, (free)

British Columbia's Trails, Rivers and Shorelines, A Status Report, Outdoor Recreation Council of British Columbia, Vancouver, 1977

Canoe Alberta A Trip Guide for Alberta's Rivers, Canoe South Book 1, Canoe South Book 2, Canoe Central, Canoe North Book 1, Canoe North Book 2, Travel Alberta, Edmonton, 1972, 1973

Canoe Routes of the Voyageurs, Eric W. Morse, Quetico Foundation of Ontario and the Minesota Historical Society, 1962

Four Lines of Defense Against Hypothermia, Queen's Printer, 1972, (free)

Health and Fitness, Health & Welfare, Canada, (free)

Man in Cold Water, The University of Victoria, Victoria, 1975

Wild Rivers, A proposal for wild scenic and recreation rivers in British Columbia, Geoff Warden & Ed Mankelow, B.C. Wildlife Federation

Wilderness Survival, Government of British Columbia Forest Service, Victoria, 1976 (free)

1976 Canada Water Year Book, Department of Fisheries and the Environment, Ottawa, 1977 (free)

Articles

B.C. Wildlife Federation, **Wild Rivers,** B.C. Outdoors, Cloverdale, April, 1974

Gregson, J.D , **Don't Fear the Tick,** British Columbia Digest, Quesnel, June, 1967

Dixon, Dean, **Tuchodi Rams,** 1975 B.C. Hunters Annual

Krueger, Jan K., **Euchiniko Sojourn,** Western Fish and Wildlife, Vancouver, September, 1974

Lomax, Harvey, **Fishin' Country,** Stuart-Trembleur-Takla Lakes, B.C. Outdoors, Cloverdale, August, 1976, **Waterway to Solitude,** B.C. Outdoors, Cloverdale, April, 1968

Malmberg, Don, **Hypothermia...Recipe for Death,** B.C. Outdoors, Cloverdale, August, 1975

Morse, Eric W., **Voyageur's Highway,** Canadian Geographical Journal, May, July, August, 1961

Parry, David, **The Great Canadian Canoe,** B.C. Outdoors, Cloverdale, April, 1974

Vanlakerveld, Frans, **Parsnip - Peace Canoe Trip,** Western Fish and Game, Vancouver, March, 1969

Wenger, Ferdi, **Canoeing the Route of the Voyageurs,** B.C. Outdoors, Cloverdale, August, October

Wright, Richard, **Adventure Route through Northern B.C.,** B.C. Outdoors, Cloverdale, June 1971, **Death of the Rivers,** Western Fish & Game, Vancouver, September, 1969, **North from British Columbia,** Western Fish & Wildlife, Vancouver, March - May - July, 1972, **The Dam,** Western Fish & Game, Vancouver, January, 1969 **The Route of the Overlanders,** Outdoor Canada, Toronto, Jan/Feb, 1977 **Trouble in the Skagit Valley,** Western Fish & Game, Vancouver, November, 1969 **Wild River,** B.C. Outdoors, Cloverdale, April 1971

Canoeing Periodicals

American Whitewater, The Journal of the American Whitewater Affiliations, Concord, N.H.

Canoe, Magazine of the American Canoe Association, The Webb Company, St. Paul, Minn.

Down River, World Publications, Mountain View, California

Canews, Recreational Canoeing Association of Canoe Sport B.C., Vancouver

INDEX

ACKNOWLEDGEMENTS

As with any guidebook of this type there are many people who have contributed to its production by sharing their favourite routes, their knowledge and experiences with us. Thankyou, to those who assisted in so many ways:

Adolph Teufele of Interior Canoe Outfitters was one of the first to offer route information, and encouragement to complete all the material. Then Robin and Suzie Sims of Cascade River Holidays shared routes, and Ron Kerr told us about canoeing in the Kootenays. Ted Underhill, author of *Berries of B.C.*, passed on information to us and Mike Chambers from Smithers.

Additional route information came from Sally Lawrence, Mr. A. Fowlie, Fred and Arlene Cameron, Rick and Wendy Antonson, W.J. McConnell, Gordon Stewart, Bob Volpert of Outdoor Adventures, Carol Conkey, Linda Melwood, and Merrily Corder.

Jim Boyd, Don Basham and Milan Jelensky of Capilano College gave us valuable information on canoeing and first aid.

We would also like to acknowledge the person who started it all, Dinty Moore, who some years ago sold us our first canoe and who has between then and now been a constant source of information, and on occasion has spared a piece of canvas for a torn skin.

All these people helped, but particular thanks must go to Alan Carter and Robin Draper of the B.C. Outdoor Recreational Council. Without their help, suggestions and information this book could not have been written. Our visits and phone calls were always met with informative, courteous and friendly response.

Finally thanks to our two sons, Richard who teethed on a canoe thwart in Quetico, and Raven who was weaned while on the Fort Nelson and Liard Rivers, and who have never complained of portages, black flies or cramped quarters between gunwales.

ABOUT THE AUTHORS...

Having ten guide books published to date, and with contributions to numerous others, this writing/photographing team is uniquely qualified to undertake preparation of this guidebook.

Rochelle Wright, a former department head nurse at the Vancouver General Hospital, has spent much of the last few years involved in research, writing and general photography. In addition to assisting in the production of television programs, she also wrote a long standing column The Outdoor Wife, for B.C. Outdoors magazine. Her photographs have appeared in such wide ranging publications as Nature Canada, The Vancouver Sun and B.C. Government publications. She continues freelancing at present.

Richard Wright, an award winning film maker, has long been involved in the communication of ideas relating to the outdoors, photography, nature and its conservation. His photographs and articles have appeared in print often, including Reader's Digest Books, Field and Stream, B.C. Outdoors, National Wildlife, Outdoor Canada and Photo Life. In addition to photographic assignments, he is working on two forthcoming books, instructs college level courses on photography, and lectures at publication seminars.

Books by these authors are:

CARIBOO MILEPOSTS

YELLOWHEAD MILEPOSTS
Volume 1: Winnipeg, Manitoba to Kamloops, British Columbia
Volume 2: Tete Jaune Cache to Prince Rupert

LOWER MAINLAND BACKROADS
Volume 1: Garibaldi to Lillooet
Volume 2: Fraser Valley
Volume 3: Hope to Clinton
Volume 4: Garibaldi Region

CANOE ROUTES BRITISH COLUMBIA

CANOE ROUTES YUKON TERRITORY

CROSS-COUNTRY SKI ROUTES BRITISH COLUMBIA

WESTERING by Richard Thomas Wright